WINDSOR CASTLE

OFFICIAL GUIDEBOOK

ROYAL COLLECTION PUBLICATIONS

Published by
Royal Collection Enterprises Ltd
St James's Palace
London SW1A 1JR

For a complete catalogue of current publications, please write to the address above, or visit our website on www.royal.gov.uk

Text written by John Martin Robinson.
This edition revised by Royal Collection Enterprises Ltd, 2004.
© 2004 Royal Collection Enterprises Ltd
Text and reproductions of all items in the Royal Collection © 2004 HM Queen Elizabeth II

120279/04/1

ISBN 1 902163 34 6

British Library Cataloguing in Publication Data
A catalogue record of this book is available from the British Library.

Designed by Baseline Arts Ltd, Oxford
Produced by Book Production Consultants plc, Cambridge
Printed and bound by Norwich Colour Print Ltd

The unique status of Windsor Castle as a working royal palace means that paintings and works of art are sometimes moved at short notice. Pictures and works of art are also frequently lent from the Royal Collection to exhibitions all over the world. The arrangement of objects and paintings may therefore occasionally vary from that given in this guidebook.

For ticket and booking information for Windsor Castle, please contact:
Ticket Sales and Information Office
Buckingham Palace
London SW1A 1AA

Credit card booking line: (+44) (0)20 7766 7304
Group bookings: (+44) (0)20 7766 7321
Fax: (+44) (0)20 7930 9625
Email: information@royalcollection.org.uk
        groupbookings@royalcollection.org.uk
        www.royal.gov.uk

RIGHT: Laurits Regner Tuxen, *The Family of Queen Victoria in 1887* (detail). The painting shows the Green Drawing Room at Windsor Castle.

FRONTISPIECE: Windsor Castle: looking up from the Lower Ward towards the Round Tower.

CONTENTS

WINDSOR CASTLE

The badge of the House of Windsor.

WINDSOR CASTLE is one of the official residences of Her Majesty Queen Elizabeth II. The Queen is Head of State of the United Kingdom of Great Britain and Northern Ireland, and Head of the Commonwealth. The Queen is also Head of State of sixteen of the Commonwealth's fifty-four member countries.

The monarch's direct powers these days are limited: as a constitutional sovereign The Queen normally acts on the advice of her ministers. Nevertheless the Government, the Judiciary and the armed services all act in The Queen's name and she is the principal symbol of national unity. The Queen is kept closely informed about all aspects of national life and the Prime Minister has a weekly audience with her. The Queen has certain residual 'prerogative' powers which include the appointment of the Prime Minister and granting the dissolution of Parliament.

Many of The Queen's duties are ceremonial and a reminder of the United Kingdom's long history. They include the State Opening of Parliament, The Queen's Birthday Parade, or Trooping the Colour as it is also known, state visits and the Garter Day celebrations, which take place at Windsor Castle.

Windsor Castle is the oldest royal residence to have remained in continuous use by the monarchs of Britain and is in many ways an architectural epitome of the history of the nation. The castle contains, as well as a royal palace, a magnificent collegiate church and the homes or workplaces of a large number of people, including the Constable and Governor of the Castle, the Military Knights of Windsor and the Dean and Canons of St George's Chapel.

The Queen is officially in residence at Windsor twice a year: in April and June. In June the annual Garter Service is held in St George's Chapel with the installation of new Knights. The castle is sometimes used as an alternative to Buckingham Palace for ceremonial visits from heads of state of other countries. The Queen and the Royal Family spend most of their private weekends at Windsor. Whenever The Queen is in residence, the Royal Standard, rather than the Union flag, is flown over the castle.

Within the state apartments at the castle are displayed works of art from the Royal Collection, many of them in the historic setting for which they were collected or commissioned by successive monarchs, notably George IV.

ILLUSTRATED TIMELINE

THIS TIMELINE SHOWS some of the most significant developments in the history of Windsor Castle from its beginnings in the 11th century to the present day.

By 1066
Royal hunting forest established at Windsor

1348
Order of the Garter founded by Edward III

1357-6:
Upper Ward reconstructed large royal pa with new St George's Hall 'Norman Gate

c.1080
Construction in earth and timber begins; present plan of the castle established

1170s
Castle largely rebuilt in stone, with square towers in a curtain wall, and the Round Tower on a motte

1220s
West wall rebuilt in stone and five round towers added to curtain wall

1240
Henry III's chapel constructed on site of present Albert Memorial Chapel in Lower Ward

NORMANDY				PLANTAGENET							
WILLIAM I	WILLIAM II	HENRY I	STEPHEN	HENRY II	RICHARD I	JOHN	HENRY III	EDWARD I	EDWARD II	EDWARD III	RICH.
1066-1087	1087-1100	1100-1135	1135-1154	1154-1189	1189-1199	1199-1216	1216-1272	1272-1307	1307-1327	1327-1377	1377

1100

1200

1300

1547
Henry VIII
buried in St
George's
Chapel

1580
Long Gallery added
by Elizabeth I to
state apartments
(now the Royal
Library)

1511
The new gate to
the Lower Ward
is constructed
under Henry VIII

1475-1528
St George's Chapel and new cloisters built

1550s
Queen Mary builds the
lodgings for the Military
Knights in the Lower Ward

LANCASTER			YORK			TUDOR				
IV	HENRY V	HENRY VI	EDWARD IV	EDWARD V	RICHARD III	HENRY VII	HENRY VIII	EDWARD VI	MARY I	ELIZABETH I
413	1413-1422	1422-1461	1461-1483	1483	1483-1485	1485-1509	1509-1547	1547-1553	1553-1558	1558-1603

toiir

400 | 1500

Joris Hoefnagel, *Windsor Castle from the north, c.1568* (detail).
This pen and ink drawing is one of the earliest known views of the castle.

7

ILLUSTRATED TIMELINE

1642-49
Windsor Castle used as a prison by Parliamentary forces

1649
Charles I buried at Windsor after execution at Whitehall

1673-84
State apartments in Upper Ward remodelled as a baroque palace. Long Walk laid out in Windsor Great Park

1823-30
Gothic reconstruction. Round Tower heightened and Grand Corridor added. New royal apartments and state apartments remodelled

1789-1806
Gothic reconstruction of state apartments begun. Frogmore House acquired and Windsor Great Park improved

STUART		COMMONWEALTH	STUART				HANOVER			
JAMES I	CHARLES I	PROTECTORATE	CHARLES II	JAMES II	WILLIAM III & MARY II	ANNE	GEORGE I	GEORGE II	GEORGE III	GEORG
1603-1625	1625-1649	1649-1659	1660-1685	1685-1688	1689-1702	1702-14	1714-1727	1727-1760	1760-1820	1820-1

1600

1700

1800

2002
Queen Elizabeth II's
Golden Jubilee

1861
Prince Albert dies at Windsor

1861-66
Lower Ward restored. Grand Staircase
to state apartments rebuilt

1911-14
State apartments refurbished

1948
Garter
Procession and
Service in
St George's
Chapel revived

1992-97
Castle restored after
serious fire damage

1845
State apartments and
Upper Ward regularly
open to the public

1977
Queen
Elizabeth II's
Silver Jubilee

		SAXE-COBURG GOTHA		WINDSOR			
IV	VICTORIA	EDWARD VII	GEORGE V	EDWARD VIII	GEORGE VI		ELIZABETH II
37	1837-1901	1901-1910	1910-1936	1936	1936-1952		1952-

1900 2000

Windsor Castle, photographed in 1860 (detail).

HISTORICAL INTRODUCTION

THE NORMAN FORTRESS

THE EXISTING VAST STRUCTURE of Windsor Castle has evolved over many centuries from its origin as a Norman fortress. It was founded by William the Conqueror as one of a chain of fortifications round London, and occupies the only naturally defensive site in this part of the Thames Valley, 30 metres (100 feet) above the river.

The earliest part of the structure is the artificial earthen mound in the middle which was raised by William the Conqueror c.1080. Norman castles were built to a standard plan with an artificial mound (motte) supporting a keep, the entrance to which was protected by a fenced yard or bailey. Windsor is the most notable example of a distinctive version of this plan, developed for use on a ridge, with baileys on both sides of a central motte.

When first built, the castle was entirely defensive, but easy access from London and proximity to an old royal hunting forest (now Windsor Great Park) soon recommended it as a royal residence. Henry I (r.1100–1135) had domestic quarters within the castle as early as 1110, and his grandson Henry II built two separate sets of apartments, a state residence in the Lower Ward, with a hall where he could entertain his court on great occasions, and a smaller residence on the north side of the Upper Ward, which was for his family's exclusive occupation.

Windsor Castle, from John Norden's *Survey* of 1607. The Round Tower is in the centre, with the Lower Ward and St George's Chapel to the right.

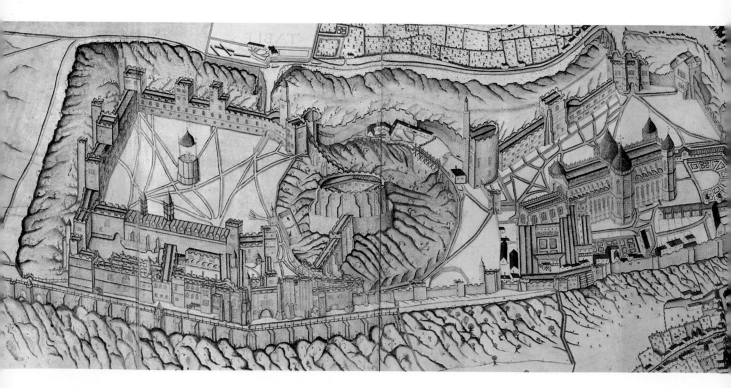

Henry II also began to replace the timber outer walls of the Upper Ward with stone. The basic curtain wall dates from his time, as does the Round Tower, built in 1170 on top of William the Conqueror's original Norman motte. The curtain wall round the Lower Ward was completed over the next sixty years. There is a well-preserved section, built by Henry III in the 1220s, with three half-round towers visible from the High Street. Henry III also rebuilt Henry II's apartments in the Lower Ward, added a new chapel, parts of which survive embedded in later structures in the Lower Ward, and improved the royal apartments in the Upper Ward.

Paul Sandby's watercolour of the Round Tower, c.1790, before Wyatville increased its height in the 1830s.

MEDIEVAL EXPANSION

THE OUTSTANDING MEDIEVAL EXPANSION of Windsor took place under Edward III (r.1327–77), when the castle was converted into a Gothic palace and the seat of the new Order of the Garter (see overleaf). The massive architecture of Windsor reflects Edward III's medieval ideal of Christian, chivalric monarchy as clearly as Louis XIV's palace at Versailles represents French seventeenth-century ideas of centralisation and the Divine Right of kings.

The Lower Ward was transformed by the building of the College of St George. Founded on 6 August 1348, the College comprised a Warden (later the Dean), twelve Canons, thirteen Priest-Vicars, four Clerks, six Choristers and a Virger. In addition there were to be twenty-six Poor Knights, to pray for the sovereign and the Knights of the Garter at daily services.

The 'Norman Gate' was built under the direction of William of Wykeham in 1357, as the principal entrance to the Upper Ward.

Reconstruction of the Upper Ward began in 1357 under the direction of William of Wykeham, Bishop of Winchester. An inner gatehouse with cylindrical towers (now misleadingly called the 'Norman Gate') was built. Stone-vaulted undercrofts, which still survive, supported extensive royal apartments on the first floor with separate rooms for the king and queen, in the tradition of English royal palaces, arranged round inner courtyards. Along the south side, facing the Quadrangle, the Great Hall and Royal Chapel were built.

Edward III's state apartments survived until the seventeenth century, hardly altered by later medieval kings. In the fifteenth century Edward IV built the present St George's Chapel to the west of Henry III's chapel. Henry VII, the first Tudor monarch, largely rebuilt the old chapel (now the Albert Memorial Chapel); he also added a new range to the west of the state apartments which Elizabeth I later extended by a Long Gallery (all now occupied by the Royal Library). Henry VIII built the entrance gateway to the Lower Ward, and his daughter Mary I built houses for the Military Knights on the south side of the Lower Ward.

The Military Knights of Windsor, photographed in the 1890s (detail).

THE ORDER OF THE GARTER

THE ORDER OF THE GARTER is one of the oldest and most important chivalric orders in the world. In January 1344, Edward III held an enormous military tournament at Windsor as a prelude to establishing an Arthurian fellowship of knights. At the time England was at war with France, and in 1348, following his victorious return from France the previous year, Edward III established the Order of the Garter, to consist of the Sovereign and 25 Knights Companion. Many of the original knights had fought with Edward III in France, and it is thought that the Garter, the emblem of the new Order, developed from a military strap or band the English knights wore during the French campaign. The patron saint of the Order was of course St George, and its motto *Honi soit qui mal y pense* ('Shame on he who thinks evil of it').

A three-day festival for the new Order was observed regularly at Windsor for two centuries, then rather less frequently. After 1674 few festivals were celebrated in their entirety. Occasional services were held until 1805, but for the rest of the 19th century the life of the Order was restricted to Chapter meetings and investitures which generally took place in London. However on 23 April 1948 King George VI ordered the Knights of the Garter to assemble at Windsor to celebrate the 600th anniversary of the founding of the Order, and the pattern of annual Garter Days at Windsor, including the procession through the castle and the service in St George's Chapel, was set. However it no longer takes place in April (when the court traditionally moved to Windsor Castle), but in June.

Today the Order of the Garter includes The Queen and members of the Royal Family as well as distinguished figures in the life of the nation.

The military connection to the Order is maintained by the Military Knights of Windsor, all of whom are retired members of the armed services, and who live within the Lower Ward of the castle. The Military Knights play an important part in the Garter Day ceremonies, and attend a service of Mattins in St George's Chapel every Sunday, representing the Knights of the Garter.

The procession of the Knights of the Garter as they make their way to St George's Chapel for the Garter ceremony.

CHARLES II'S BAROQUE PALACE

DURING THE ENGLISH CIVIL WAR of 1642–49 the castle was seized by Parliamentary forces who used it as a prison. King Charles I was buried in St George's Chapel after his execution at Whitehall in 1649.

On the Restoration of the monarchy in 1660 Charles II determined to reinstate Windsor as his principal non-metropolitan palace. The architect Hugh May was appointed in 1673 to supervise the work, which took eleven years to complete. May retained the blocky, castellated appearance of the buildings but regularised their exterior and inserted round-arched windows, some of which are still visible today.

The interior of the castle was a rich contrast to its exterior and contained the grandest baroque state apartments in England. The arrangement of duplicated sets of rooms for the king and queen was kept but expanded. The walls were panelled in oak and festooned with brilliant carvings by the virtuoso English woodcarver Grinling Gibbons (1648–1721) and his assistant Henry Phillips. The ceilings were painted by Antonio Verrio (c.1640–1707), an Italian artist brought to Windsor from Paris by the 1st Duke of Montagu. Only those in the Queen's Presence and Audience Chambers and the King's Dining Room have survived, but the general form and proportions of the state apartments today are still as created by Charles II.

Charles II, a fragment of Verrio's lost painted ceiling from St George's Hall.

Wenceslaus Hollar, *Bird's-eye view of Windsor Castle*, 1672 (detail). The castle before the alterations made for Charles II by Hugh May.

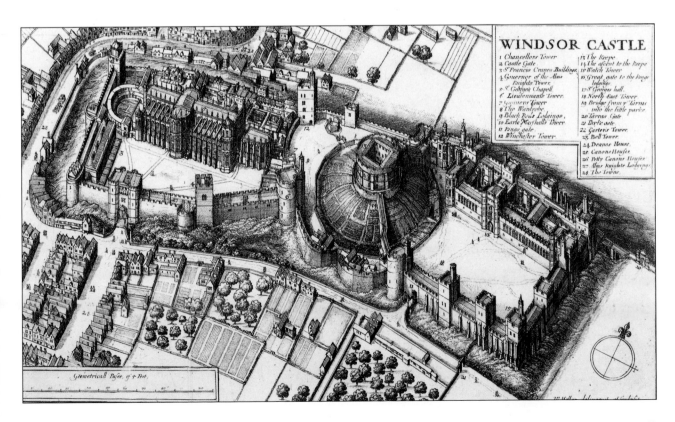

THE EAST FRONT OF THE CASTLE, showing the East Terrace garden, laid out for George IV in the 1820s.

PICTURESQUE REVIVAL

WILLIAM III AND THE EARLY HANOVERIAN KINGS preferred the palace of Hampton Court to Windsor; but George III chose it as his favourite residence, and after his recovery from his first attack of porphyria in 1789, decided to move to Windsor. He initiated extensive renovations, designed by James Wyatt, who began to convert Hugh May's round-arched windows to the more fashionable Gothic style, and to lighten the appearance of the state rooms by replacing the oak panelling with coloured fabrics. At the same time a new state entrance and Gothic staircase were constructed.

When George IV inherited the throne in 1820, he determined to continue the Gothic transformation of the castle and the creation of comfortable and splendid new royal apartments. In this he was strongly influenced by his chief artistic adviser, Sir Charles Long. It was decided in 1823 to hold a limited competition for the work and Long drew up an informal brief. Its principal points were the heightening of Henry II's Round Tower, the general

enhancement of the silhouette of the castle, with extra towers and battlements, the addition of the Grand Corridor round the Upper Ward, the creation of the Waterloo Chamber to celebrate the Allied victory over Napoleon in 1815, the continuation up to the castle of the Long Walk laid out by Charles II, and the making of the King George IV Gateway. Three leading architects, Sir John Soane, Sir Robert Smirke and John Nash, were asked to submit plans, as was the late James Wyatt's nephew Jeffry, who was awarded the task. He carried out Long's programme to the last detail, creating the present appearance of the Upper Ward, earning a knighthood and medievalising his surname to Wyatville. Inside the castle new private rooms were made as a setting for George IV's magnificent art collection, and the old hall and chapel were knocked together to create the vast, Gothic-revival St George's Hall. Charles II's state rooms were refurbished, this work continuing (still under Wyatville's direction) into the reign of William IV. George IV himself took up residence in the castle in 1828.

Joseph Nash, *Sunday morning in the Lower Ward*, 1846. St George's Chapel is on the left, and the houses of the Military Knights of Windsor, built by Mary I, can be seen on the right, stretching up the south side of the Lower Ward.

QUEEN VICTORIA AT WINDSOR

IN MANY WAYS WINDSOR CASTLE reached its apogee in the reign of Queen Victoria. She spent the greater part of every year at Windsor, and in her reign it enjoyed the position of principal palace of the British monarchy and focus of the British Empire, as well as that of nearly the whole of royal Europe, many members of which were related to the Queen. The castle was visited by heads of state from all over the world, and on these occasions the state rooms were used for their original purpose by royal guests.

Wyatville and George IV had left the castle in such splendid order that no major work was required. Queen Victoria made a few minor alterations, reconstructing the Grand Staircase and creating a new private chapel (destroyed in the fire of 1992) to the design of Edward Blore. In the Lower Ward the Curfew Tower and Horseshoe Cloisters were both restored, and the disused chapel east of St George's was remodelled with marble and mosaic as a memorial to Prince Albert, who died at Windsor Castle on 14 December 1861.

ABOVE LEFT: Prince and Princess Frederick William of Prussia, photographed on the East Terrace at Windsor Castle in January 1858 (detail). Queen Victoria's eldest daughter, the Princess Royal, married Prince Frederick William of Prussia in 1858. Frederick was the grandson of Frederick William IV of Prussia, and father of Wilhelm II, 'Kaiser Wilhelm' of the First World War. Queen Victoria was thus grandmother to the man who many in 1914 saw as Britain's most dangerous enemy.

ABOVE RIGHT: Queen Victoria and Princess Louise with a bust of the Prince Consort, photographed by William Bambridge in March 1862 (detail). Prince Albert's early death, at the age of 42, was the greatest tragedy of Queen Victoria's life. Her seclusion in mourning for many years after led to her becoming known as the 'Widow of Windsor'.

RIGHT: Three of Queen Victoria and Prince Albert's children, Prince Arthur, Princess Helena and Princess Louise, photographed in fancy dress at Windsor in 1856 (detail). Prince Arthur wears the uniform of a guardsman in the Grenadier Guards.

TOP: A gun installed on the East Terrace at Windsor Castle, photographed between 1914 and 1918.

ABOVE: The Great Kitchen at Windsor Castle, photographed by Roger Fenton in 1878.

RIGHT: Vaults being dug in the North Terrace in 1883 to house the generators bringing an electricity supply to the castle (detail).

FROM THE FIRE OF 1992 TO THE PRESENT DAY

FOR MOST OF THE TWENTIETH CENTURY the castle survived as it was in the nineteenth century, even coming through various bombing raids in the Second World War relatively unscathed. But on 20 November 1992 a serious fire broke out in Queen Victoria's private chapel at the north-east angle of the Upper Ward. It is thought to have been caused by a spotlight igniting a curtain high up over the altar. Despite the efforts of the castle staff and the fire brigade, the fire spread rapidly at roof level, destroying the ceilings of George IV's St George's Hall and Grand Reception Room as well as gutting the Royal Family's private chapel, the State Dining Room, the Crimson Drawing Room and various subsidiary rooms. By great good fortune the rooms worst affected by the fire were empty at the time as they were in the course of being rewired. As a result very few of the castle's artistic treasures were destroyed. The principal casualties were a sideboard and a painting, *George III at a review* by Sir William Beechey, both of which were too big to move.

Repair and restoration began immediately after the fire. Two committees were set up to supervise the work – a general Restoration Committee, chaired by The Duke of Edinburgh; and an Art and Design Committee, which was chaired

ABOVE: Her Majesty The Queen inspecting the damage in St George's Hall after the fire of November 1992.

BELOW: The Brunswick Tower outlined against the fire in the Upper Ward.

A craftsman at work restoring the gold-leaf on the panelling of the fire-damaged Grand Reception Room. Over 3,000 square metres of gilding (11,000 square feet) was needed to restore the state apartments.

The Jubilee Garden at Windsor Castle, looking up toward St George's Gate. The bandstand is on the right, and visitors turn left at St George's Gate to reach the Round Tower and the route to the state apartments.

by The Prince of Wales. The damaged rooms were restored to the original George IV and Wyatville designs, but those areas which had been totally destroyed – including the old private chapel, the Holbein Room and the roof of St George's Hall – were rebuilt to harmonious new designs by Giles Downes of the Sidell Gibson Partnership, who were chosen out of a short-list of four architects. Their aim was to create a modern Gothic style, original in its detail, but continuing in a long English tradition stretching back almost without break to the Middle Ages. The Lantern Lobby is the principal new interior in this style in the castle, and is notable for its fine proportions and the ingenious handling of space to create interesting vistas and connections, as well as for its superb craftsmanship.

A further new development has been the creation of the Jubilee Garden, designed by Tom Stuart-Smith, to celebrate the Golden Jubilee of Her Majesty The Queen. The Jubilee Garden stretches from the main visitors' entrance to St George's Gate on Castle Hill, and is the first garden to have been created at the castle since the 1820s. It takes its inspiration both from the castle's historic parkland landscape and from the picturesque architectural style introduced at Windsor by Sir Jeffry Wyatville. The trees in the garden echo those found in its park, such as beech, lime, holm oak and robinia, while a large shrubbery on the south side contains plants such as lilacs, philadelphus, viburnums and magnolias, all typical of the shrubbery plantations of the time of George IV.

At the centre of the garden a stone bandstand is the setting for regular performances by the bands of the Household Division. The bandstand repeats in its decoration the image of the Garter Star – a motif which the visitor encounters throughout the castle.

TOUR OF THE CASTLE

VISITORS MAKE THEIR WAY to the state apartments in the Upper Ward, walking past the Round Tower on its steep artificial motte. The moat protecting the Tower has always been dry, and as visitors will see, is now the enchanting garden of the Governor of Windsor Castle, whose official residence adjoins the 'Norman Gate' at the top of Middle Ward.

Entrance to the state apartments is via the North Terrace, which was originally constructed by Henry VIII, then widened by Charles II. It has magnificent views over the Thames Valley to Eton, with the wooded Buckinghamshire landscape beyond. The white-painted house in the middle distance is Stoke Park, which was designed by James Wyatt for John Penn, grandson of the founder of Pennsylvania.

Before entering the state apartments, visitors can also see Queen Mary's Dolls' House, in its specially designed room, and France and Marianne, the two dolls presented to The Queen and Princess Margaret in 1938 by the children of France, following the State Visit to France of King George VI and Queen Elizabeth.

During the winter months it is also possible to visit the Semi-State Rooms, created for George IV in the 1820s. At other times of the year these rooms are used by The Queen for official entertaining. This part of the castle was severely damaged by the fire of 1992, and access to the Semi-State Rooms is via the Lantern Lobby, where the fire began (page 58).

LEFT: Paul Sandby, *The North Terrace looking west*, c.1780.

RIGHT: Queen Alexandra, photographed on the South Terrace at Windsor Castle in January 1906. The photograph has been attributed to her daughter Princess Victoria of Wales.

THE UPPER WARD AND NORTH TERRACE

LEFT: Queen Mary's Dolls' House exhibition room was also designed by Lutyens. The Pilkington glass case was made for the Ideal Home Exhibition of 1925, and presented to Windsor Castle by the *Daily Mail* for the permanent protection of the dolls' house.

BELOW: A Wisden cricket bat from Queen Mary's Dolls' House, set against a full-size cricket ball to give an idea of scale.

QUEEN MARY'S DOLLS' HOUSE

THIS FAMOUS DOLLS' HOUSE was given to Queen Mary in 1924. It was designed by Sir Edwin Lutyens and nearly every item in it was specially commissioned on the tiny scale of one to twelve. It was intended as an accurate record of contemporary domestic design, and has become one of the most celebrated dolls' houses in the world. It has running water, electric light and power, the tiny gramophone plays and the bottles in the wine cellar contain genuine vintage wines.

The furniture and other contents were made by leading manufacturers of the day, while the garden was designed by Gertrude Jekyll. The paintings were commissioned from well-known artists and the books on the shelves of the dolls' house Library are all by prominent authors, some written in their own hand. Rudyard Kipling, G. K. Chesterton, Sir Arthur Conan Doyle, Thomas Hardy and J. M. Barrie are among the writers represented.

In the adjoining room France and Marianne are displayed, with some of their remarkable trousseaux of miniature clothes and accessories by such leading Parisian fashion houses as Worth, Lanvin, Cartier, Hermès and Vuitton.

ABOVE: France (on the left) and Marianne, wearing some of their Parisian trousseaux.

Separate publications are available on both Queen Mary's Dolls' House and on France and Marianne.

THE GALLERY

THE VISITOR NOW ENTERS a vaulted undercroft, originally created by James Wyatt and extended by Jeffry Wyatville as the principal entrance to the state apartments. When the Grand Staircase was changed under Queen Victoria, this area was separated from the state apartments, and now houses special exhibitions from the Royal Collection, including works from the Photograph Collection and the Royal Archives, and Old Master drawings from the exceptional collection in the Royal Library.

LEFT: G. Thomas, *Queen Victoria and Napoleon III in the State Entrance*, 1855

ABOVE: Rockingham dessert plate from the China Museum.

THE CHINA MUSEUM

THE CHINA MUSEUM houses magnificent china services from leading English and European porcelain manufacturers of the 18th and 19th centuries, including Sèvres, Tournai, Meissen, Copenhagen, Naples, Rockingham and Worcester. These are still used for royal banquets and other important occasions.

The carved Ionic capitals at the top of the columns in this room survive from Hugh May's programme of rebuilding for Charles II.

DISPLAY CABINETS
(anti-clockwise from the entrance)

Royal Copenhagen dessert service, presented to King Edward VII and Queen Alexandra in 1863 by the ladies of Denmark.

Fürstenberg service c.1773. Presented to George III by his brother-in-law, the Duke of Brunswick.

Etruscan service, Naples, 1785–7. Presented to George III by Ferdinand IV, King of Naples, in 1787.

Rockingham service, 1830–33. Commissioned by William IV in 1830.

Staffordshire (Daniel) service, c.1826–30. Made for the Duke of Clarence (later William IV).

Worcester service, 1830. Commissioned by William IV in 1830.

Worcester Harlequin service, c.1807-16. Made for George IV.

Coalport service, 1818. Presented to Edward, Duke of Kent, by the City of London on his marriage.

Tournai service, c.1787. Made for the duc d'Orléans. Acquired by George IV between 1803 and 1807.

Sèvres service, 1764–70. Acquired by George IV.

Examples from several Meissen porcelain services, c.1750.

Flora Danica service, Copenhagen, 1863. Presented to King Edward VII and Queen Alexandra on their wedding.

THE STATE APARTMENTS

THE GRAND STAIRCASE

ROOM PLAN →

THE GRAND STAIRCASE is the third to have been built here since the restoration of the castle was begun by George III in the late eighteenth century. James Wyatt originally constructed a staircase in the space now occupied by the Grand Vestibule. Wyatville removed this and built a new staircase on the present site by roofing over the medieval Brick Court. This arrangement, in turn, was considered inconvenient and the present staircase, on a reversed alignment, was created in 1866. It is now a magnificent and fitting entrance to the castle, filled with light from an immense glazed timber lantern overhead.

The walls of the Grand Staircase are lined with trophies of arms, based on an arrangement originally worked out by Sir Samuel Rush Meyrick, who was knighted by William IV for his services. The over life-size marble statue of George IV on the half-landing survives from Wyatville's design and commemorates the monarch who is largely responsible for the present appearance of Windsor Castle.

THE GRAND VESTIBULE

ROOM PLAN →

THE GRAND VESTIBULE is dominated by a statue of Queen Victoria by Sir Joseph Boehm (1871). Its handsome plaster fan vault, with naturalistic foliage bosses and angels, was executed by Francis Bernasconi, a plasterer of genius who first worked at Windsor under James Wyatt, and continued under Wyatville. The glazed Gothic showcases round the sides of the room, made in 1888 to display Queen Victoria's Golden Jubilee presents, now contain a collection of arms, including trophies from the conquest of Seringapatam in India in 1799 and from the Napoleonic Wars – not least the lead bullet that killed Nelson at Trafalgar in 1805.

LEFT: The Grand Staircase, with Sir Francis Chantrey's statue of George IV.

RIGHT: The bullet which killed Lord Nelson on the deck of H.M.S. Victory during the Battle of Trafalgar, 1805.

THE GRAND STAIRCASE

▨ SCULPTURE

1 Over life-size statue of George IV by Sir Francis Chantrey, 1828–32. Copied from Chantrey's bronze statue of the king at Brighton.

▨ ARMS & ARMOUR

2 Colours of disbanded Irish and English regiments.

3 Trophies and suits of armour, 16th–19th centuries.

4 Child's armour made for Henry, Prince of Wales. Greenwich, c.1610.

5 Child's armour made for Henry, Prince of Wales. Probably French, c.1610.

THE GRAND VESTIBULE

▨ PICTURES

1 David Morier, *George II on horseback*, c.1745

2 John Vanderbank, *George I on horseback*, 1726

▨ FURNITURE

3 Range of fitted oak cases, made to display Queen Victoria's Golden Jubilee presents, 1887–9 and later rearranged to display Oriental and European arms and relics.

▨ ARMS & ARMOUR (IN DISPLAY CABINETS)

4 Arms and armour and relics of Tipú Sultán, King of Mysore (c.1749–99), including the gold tiger from his throne taken at the Siege of Seringapatam in 1799.

5 Oriental arms and trophies, including an Inca crown and an Ethiopian crown, c.1840.

6 European firearms, including sporting guns, mainly 18th century.

7 Trophy of swords, European, 17th–18th centuries.

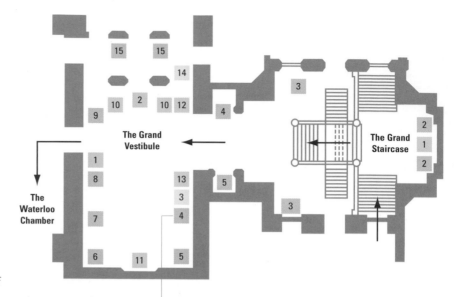

Gold tiger's head from the throne of Tipú Sultán.

8 European arms including French pistols and a sword by N.-N. Boutet; the travelling service of Stephanie de Beauharnais, the adopted daughter of Napoleon, made by Biennais, Paris, 1798–1809; Napoleon's scarlet cloak, captured at Waterloo; and the bullet that killed Lord Nelson at Trafalgar in 1805.

9 Three embroidered velvet cloaks and a surcoat and stole made for George IV, reputedly used at his Coronation in Hanover in 1821; and a group of sabretaches and pouches from Hussar regiments.

▨ SCULPTURE

10 Marble busts of Charles I and William III, early 18th century. Acquired by Queen Elizabeth, consort of King George VI, in 1937.

11 Marble statue of Queen Victoria with her collie, Sharp, by Sir J. E. Boehm, 1871.

12 Adrian de Vries, bronze plaque representing Rudolph II introducing the Liberal Arts into Bohemia, 1609. Purchased by George IV.

13 Benvenuto Cellini, bronze model of a standing satyr for the Porte Dorée, Fontainebleau, c.1542.

THE LOBBY TO THE GRAND VESTIBULE

▨ FURNITURE

14 Leather-covered sedan chair with gilt-metal decoration, late 18th century. The chair originally belonged to Queen Charlotte, and was acquired by Queen Victoria in 1883 from the Duke of Teck.

▨ ARMS & ARMOUR (IN DISPLAY CABINETS)

15 Two cases containing equipment of the 10th Light Dragoons, including a jacket and helmet belonging to George IV as Colonel of the Regiment (1793–1819).

RIGHT: The Grand Vestibule.

THE ANTE-THRONE ROOM

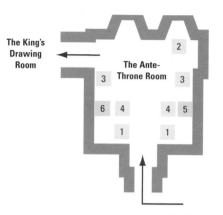

The King's Drawing Room ←

The Ante-Throne Room

↑ (The Waterloo Chamber)

THIS SMALL ROOM IS MUCH REDUCED from its seventeenth-century dimensions when it was the King's Audience Chamber. The King's chair of state stood here until the reign of George III. Wyatville reduced the room in size and turned it into an ante-room. Today it marks the approximate divide between the part of the castle remodelled in the reign of George IV to make larger and grander reception rooms, and Charles II's smaller state apartments. The latter still retain their old layout and proportions and some of their seventeenth-century character and architectural detail, though Wyatville replaced all except three of the painted ceilings Verrio created for Charles II on the grounds that they were irreparably damaged. However the carved oak cornice in this room, decorated with acanthus leaves, does survive from Grinling Gibbons' work for Charles II.

FURNITURE

1 Pair of giltwood mirrors (originally picture frames), carved with the cyphers of William III and Mary II.

2 Rosewood and brass-inlaid centre table, early 19th century.

3 Settee and chairs by Morel & Seddon, c.1828. The firm of Morel & Seddon were used extensively by George IV in his re-furbishing of Windsor Castle.

4 Pair of ebony and Boulle marquetry side cabinets, mid-19th century.

TAPESTRIES

Two tapestries from the *History of Meleager*, woven at the Gobelins factory between 1824 and 1833, and presented to Queen Victoria by King Louis-Philippe in 1843.

5 The Hunt

6 The Death of Meleager

The Waterloo Chamber

The visitor passes through this vast room, created by Wyatville by roofing over the former Horn Court, on the way to the King's and Queen's state apartments. It was designed to display Sir Thomas Lawrence's portraits of the Allied leaders responsible for the defeat of Napoleon. That of the Duke of Wellington is best viewed at this point on the tour.

There is an opportunity to inspect the room and the pictures in more detail later in the tour; see page 75.

LEFT: Sir Thomas Lawrence, *Arthur Wellesley, 1st Duke of Wellington*, 1814–15

THE KING'S DRAWING ROOM

ROOM PLAN →

IN CHARLES II'S TIME THIS WAS THE THIRD ROOM IN THE KING'S APARTMENT

GEORGE IV'S BODY LAY IN STATE IN THIS ROOM AFTER HIS DEATH IN 1830

QUEEN VICTORIA OCCASIONALLY USED THIS ROOM FOR PRIVATE THEATRICAL PERFORMANCES

THE KING'S DRAWING ROOM and the following rooms are Charles II's additions to the castle, partly redecorated in the late eighteenth and early nineteenth centuries. Today they are mainly used for the display of works of art from the Royal Collection.

In the nineteenth century the King's Drawing Room was known as the Rubens Room from the paintings by Rubens and his school which still hang here today. Prince Albert developed the theme of hanging particular groups of paintings in particular rooms, as the visitor will see while going round the state apartments.

Wyatville's geometrical plaster ceiling, embellished with the arms of George IV and the Garter Star, replaced one of Verrio's most ambitious paintings, showing Charles II triumphant in a chariot, scattering his enemies. It was one of a series of thirteen painted ceilings that celebrated the Restoration of the English monarchy in 1660. All had fulsomely Royalist subjects, and were influenced by Charles Lebrun's work for Louis XIV at Versailles.

However the seventeenth-century cornice by Grinling Gibbons with crisply carved acanthus leaves survives, as do the waist-height panelled dado and 8-panelled doors. George III replaced the oak panels higher on the walls with bright fabric. In his time it was Garter blue material; William IV changed it to crimson damask. The early nineteenth-century Siena marble chimneypiece was designed by Wyatville, who also added the large bay window from which there is a fine view over Eton.

Sir Peter Paul Rubens, *Winter: Interior of a barn*, 1620–30

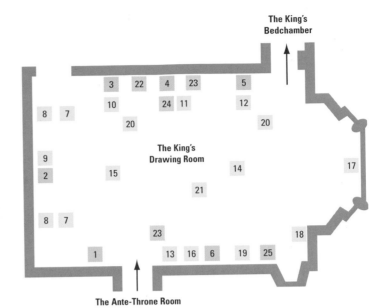

**The King's
Bedchamber**

**The King's
Drawing Room**

The Ante-Throne Room

PICTURES

1 Studio of Sir Peter Paul Rubens, *Equestrian portrait of Philip II of Spain*, c.1620

2 Studio of Sir Peter Paul Rubens, *Portrait of a gentleman on horseback*, c.1610

3 Sir Peter Paul Rubens, *Winter: Interior of a barn*, 1620–30

4 Sir Peter Paul Rubens, *The Holy Family with St Francis*, 1626–8 (overmantel)

5 Sir Peter Paul Rubens, *Summer landscape with peasants going to market*, 1620–30

6 Sir Anthony Van Dyck, *St Martin dividing his cloak*, c.1618–20

FURNITURE

7 Pair of Boulle and lacquer cabinets, 18th and 19th centuries.

8 Two oval carved and giltwood pier glasses designed by John Yenn, c.1794–5, and carved by Richard Lawrence.

9 Pollard elm and giltwood writing table by Jacob Frères, c.1805.

10 French lacquer and gilt-bronze cabinet, late 18th and 19th centuries.

11 Pair of English giltwood torchères, c.1730.

12 French lacquer and gilt-bronze cabinet by J. Baumhauer, c.1770. Acquired by George IV in 1825.

13 Set of four baroque giltwood torchères, c.1840.

14 French ebony and Boulle marquetry writing table, c.1710.

15 Giltwood seat furniture by Morel & Seddon, c.1828.

16 English giltwood seat furniture with covers embroidered by Frederica, Duchess of York. Acquired by George IV in 1827.

17 Organ-clock by Charles Clay, c.1730, incorporating a rock crystal and enamel casket made by Melchior Baumgartner in Augsburg, 1664. It now contains the Bible of the Victorian military hero General Gordon of Khartoum (1833–85).

18 French ebony and lacquer secretaire, early 19th century.

19 French ebony veneered writing desk, late 18th century.

20 Pair of 18th-century gilt-bronze allegorical groups representing Painting and Sculpture. Purchased by George IV in 1827.

21 Persian carpet, early 20th century. Presented to King Edward VII by the Shah of Persia in 1903.

PORCELAIN

22 Four Chinese blue and white porcelain jars and covers, 17th century.

23 Four candelabra of Chinese blue porcelain with French gilt-bronze mounts, 18th century.

24 Garniture of Chinese celadon porcelain vases, mid-18th century.

SCULPTURE

25 Bronze figure of *Hercules* after Giambologna, ?18th century.

THE KING'S BEDCHAMBER

UNDER GEORGE III, CHANGES SIMILAR to those in the King's Drawing Room were made to this room. The seventeenth-century wainscot was removed from the walls, which were then hung with crimson cloth (recently renewed in damask). Wyatville also replaced Verrio's painted ceiling, installing a plaster composition incorporating the Stuart royal arms and the date 1660 to commemorate the Restoration. Grinling Gibbons' excellent carved cornice was retained. Today the room is dominated by a magnificent bed, attributed to the French cabinet-maker Georges Jacob, and acquired by George IV. Its present hangings of green and purple record the State Visit of the Emperor Napoleon III in 1855. His initials and those of his Empress, Eugénie, are embroidered on the foot of the bed. The Emperor was invested with the Order of the Garter by Queen Victoria while he was at Windsor. The room also includes works from George III's collection of Canalettos, and a fireplace designed by Sir William Chambers and brought here from Buckingham House while it was being remodelled as Buckingham Palace.

Canaletto, *Venice: The Bacino di S. Marco on Ascension Day*, c.1733–4

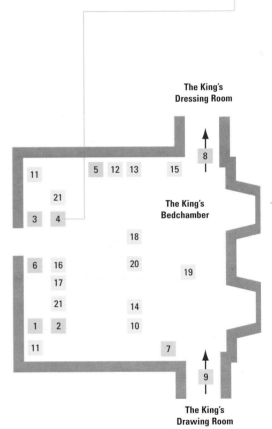

PICTURES

1 Canaletto, *Venice: Caprice view of the Piazzetta with the Horses of S. Marco*, 1743

2 Canaletto, *Venice: A regatta on the Grand Canal*, c.1733

3 Canaletto, *Venice: The Colleoni Monument in a caprice setting*, 1744

4 Canaletto, *Venice: The Bacino di S. Marco on Ascension Day*, c.1733–4

5 Canaletto, *Venice: The Grand Canal with S. Maria della Salute*, 1744

6 Thomas Gainsborough, *Johann Christian Fischer*, c.1774

7 Francis Cotes, *Queen Charlotte with Charlotte, Princess Royal*, 1767

Over Doors

8 Canaletto, *Venice: Caprice view of the Molo and the Doge's Palace*, c.1743

9 Canaletto, *Venice: Caprice view of the courtyard of the Doge's Palace with the Scala dei Giganti*, 1744

FURNITURE

10 French giltwood 'polonaise' bed, attributed to Georges Jacob, late 18th century.

11 Pair of French corner cupboards with Japanese lacquer panels and gilt-bronze mounts, by Bernard (II) van Risamburgh, c.1750.

12 French chest of drawers with Japanese lacquer panels and gilt-bronze mounts, by Bernard (II) van Risamburgh, c.1750.

13 French patinated and gilt-bronze 'Rape of Europa' clock; case by R. Osmond, later movement by B. L. Vulliamy, on a musical-box base, mid-18th century.

14 French oval parquetry table by R. Lacroix, c.1770, inset with Sèvres porcelain plaque dated 1763.

15 Part of a large set of English carved and gilt gesso side chairs, c.1730.

16 Gilt-bronze and white marble allegorical clock by Vulliamy, 1787, with Derby porcelain figure.

17 Pair of French white marble and gilt-bronze vases, late 18th century.

18 Regency rosewood games table, early 19th century.

The King's Dressing Room

The King's Bedchamber

The King's Drawing Room

19 French (Savonnerie) carpet, second half of the 18th century.

20 Cut-glass chandelier, early 19th century.

21 Pair of French patinated and gilt-bronze candelabra by F. Rémond. Of the same model as those made in 1783 for the apartments of the comte d'Artois at Versailles. Acquired by George IV.

LEFT: THE KING'S BEDCHAMBER. Charles II used this room only for the official ceremony of the Levée (rising, resting and receiving guests).

THE KING'S DRESSING ROOM

THIS ROOM CONTAINS SOME OF THE FINEST SMALLER PAINTINGS IN THE ROYAL COLLECTION

CHARLES II SLEPT IN THIS ROOM, RATHER THAN IN THE KING'S OFFICIAL BEDCHAMBER

ABOVE: Lucas Cranach the Elder, *Apollo and Diana*, c.1530

ON DISPLAY IN THIS ROOM are some of the most important northern Renaissance paintings in the Royal Collection, most dating from the sixteenth century. Over the fireplace is the Dutch artist Marten van Heemskerck's *The Four Last Things*, dated 1565. The title refers to Death, Judgement, Paradise and Hell depicted in the painting. Amongst the paintings on the wall opposite the windows are two small portraits by Hans Holbein the Younger, who was in the service of King Henry VIII, and three by his German compatriot Lucas Cranach the Elder. The most famous painting in the room is Pieter Bruegel the Elder's *The Massacre of the Innocents* on the right-hand wall. It depicts the story from St Matthew's Gospel in which King Herod decreed that all the newborn children of Bethlehem be slaughtered. The artist has set the story in his own time and country, and Herod's soldiers resemble those of the Imperial army. The composition was altered in the seventeenth century, presumably for a squeamish owner, so that the infant children were painted over and the subject transformed into the sacking of a village.

The carved wooden cornice by Grinling Gibbons and the panelled dado again survive from the time of Charles II, but here, as in the other state rooms, the walls were stripped of wainscot and hung with crimson cloth by George III.

William IV eliminated the old painted ceiling and installed the existing moulded plaster design sporting his own monogram and arms, while the anchors and tridents recall his career in the Navy before he ascended the throne.

RIGHT: Jan Gossaert, called Mabuse, *The children of Christian II of Denmark*, c.1526

Pieter Bruegel the Elder, *The Massacre of the Innocents*, c.1565–7

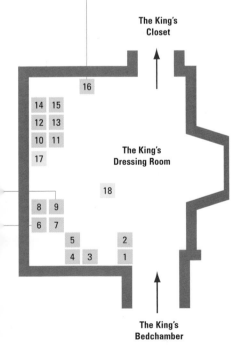

The King's Closet

The King's Dressing Room

The King's Bedchamber

■ **PICTURES**

1 Jean Clouet, *Portrait of a man holding a volume of Petrarch*, c.1530

2 Hans Memlinc, *Portrait of a man*, c.1480

3 Marten van Heemskerck, *The Four Last Things*, 1565

4 Hans Holbein the Younger, *William Reskimer*, c.1532–3

5 Albrecht Dürer, *Burkhard von Speyer*, 1506

6 Lucas Cranach the Elder, *Apollo and Diana*, c.1530

7 Jan Breugel the Elder, *Adam and Eve in the Garden of Eden*, 1615

8 Quinten Metsys, *Desiderius Erasmus*, 1517

9 Jan Gossaert, called Mabuse, *The children of Christian II of Denmark*, c.1526

10 Hans Holbein the Younger, *Derich Born*, 1533

11 Hendrick van Steenwyck the Younger, *The Liberation of St Peter*, 1619

12 Hans Baldung Grien, *Portrait of young man with a Rosary*, 1509

13 Lucas Cranach the Elder, *The Judgement of Paris*, c.1538–43

14 Lucas Cranach the Elder, *Lucretia*, 1530

15 Jan Breugel the Elder, *A Flemish Fair*, 1600

16 Pieter Bruegel the Elder, *The Massacre of the Innocents*, c.1565–7

■ **FURNITURE**

17 French mahogany trellis-back chairs and settee by Georges Jacob, late 18th century.

18 English gilt-bronze chandelier, early 19th century.

THE KING'S CLOSET

THE KING'S CLOSET WAS CREATED out of two smaller rooms by James Wyatt in 1804. Here again the seventeenth-century cornice and dado survive (or have been copied), but the wall panels gave way to more cheerful hangings in the reign of George III and the present ceiling is of moulded plaster to Wyatville's design. It is dated 1833 and displays the monogram and arms of Adelaide of Saxe-Meiningen, Queen Consort of King William IV.

Agnolo Bronzino,
*Portrait of a lady
in green*, c.1530

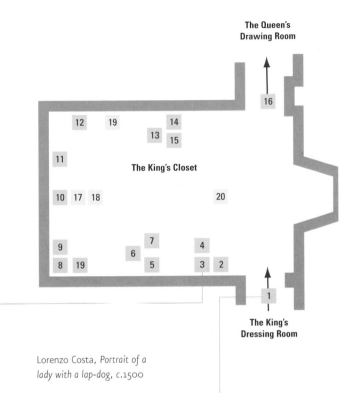

Lorenzo Costa, *Portrait of a lady with a lap-dog, c.1500*

PICTURES

1 Dosso Dossi, *Saint William*, c.1524

2 Palma Vecchio, *A sibyl*, c.1520

3 Lorenzo Costa, *Portrait of a lady with a lap-dog*, c.1500

4 Attributed to Raphael, *Self-portrait*, c.1506

5 Girolamo Savoldo, *The Virgin Adoring the Child with Two Donors*, c.1525

6 Andrea del Sarto, *The Virgin and Child*, c.1528–30

7 Giovanni Bellini, *Portrait of a young man*, c.1507

8 Attributed to Lorenzo Lotto, *Portrait of a man holding a glove*, c.1520

9 Correggio, *The Holy Family with Saint Jerome*, c.1517

10 Dosso Dossi, *The Holy Family*, c.1528–29

11 Agnolo Bronzino, *Portrait of a lady in green*, c.1530

12 Jacopo Bassano, *The Journey of Jacob*, c.1560

13 Francesco Salviati, *The Virgin and Child with an Angel*, c.1555

14 Parmigianino, *Pallas Athene*, c.1531–35

15 Benozzo Gozzoli, *The Fall of Simon Magus*, 1461

16 Giovanni Cariani, *The lovers*, c.1517

FURNITURE

17 French lacquer cabinet with gilt-bronze mounts, 1775 and later.

18 Bronze equestrian group of Marcus Aurelius, 18th century, after the Antique.

19 French mahogany trellis-back chairs by Georges Jacob, late 18th century.

20 English gilt-bronze chandelier, c.1830.

Dosso Dossi, *Saint William*, c.1524

THE QUEEN'S DRAWING ROOM

ROOM PLAN →

AS AT HAMPTON COURT PALACE near Richmond, the King's and Queen's state apartments at Windsor Castle adjoin at right angles. All the rooms in the Queen's Apartment survive, except the Bedchamber, which is now part of the adjoining Royal Library and is not open to the public. The visitor sees them in the reverse of their original order.

The chief characteristic of the Queen's Drawing Room today is the display of some of the finest sixteenth- and seventeenth-century portraits from the Royal Collection, including a number of works by Hans Holbein.

The Queen's Drawing Room was originally hung with tapestry and Verrio's ceiling was painted with an assembly of the gods. In 1834 Wyatville remodelled the room (except the dado and cornice) to match the King's Apartment. His plaster ceiling with its broad mouldings and naturalistic foliage was intended to create a neo-Carolean effect. The arms in the ceiling are those of King William IV and Queen Adelaide. The large panes of glass in the windows are among the earliest plate glass in England, while the gilt-bronze chandelier was commissioned for the castle by George IV.

Visitors now make a detour from the Queen's Apartment to the King's Dining Room. This takes them through the area of the Octagon Lobby, with its oak panels and limewood carvings, including oval reliefs of the heads of saints which originally came from the old Royal Chapel.

Robert Peake,
*Henry, Prince of
Wales, in the hunting
field*, c.1605

■ PICTURES

1 Marcus Gheeraerts the Younger, *Anne of Denmark*, 1614

2 Hans Holbein the Younger, *Sir Henry Guildford*, 1527

3 Joos van Cleve, *Henry VIII*, c.1535

4 Girolamo da Treviso, *A Protestant allegory*, c.1536

5 Attributed to Guillim Scrots, *Edward VI*, c.1546

6 Robert Peake, *Henry Prince of Wales in the hunting field*, c.1606–7

7 Attributed to Guillim Scrots, *Elizabeth I when Princess*, c.1546

8 Hans Eworth, *Henry Stewart, Lord Darnley, and his brother Charles Stewart, Earl of Lennox*, c.1562

9 Attributed to Hans Eworth, *Elizabeth I and the Three Goddesses*, 1569

10 Hans Holbein the Younger, *Thomas Howard, 3rd Duke of Norfolk*, 1538–9

11 William Wissing, *William III*, c.1685

12 Paul van Somer, *James I*, c.1620

13 John Riley, *Prince George of Denmark*, c.1687

14 Studio of Daniel Mytens, *Ludovick Stuart, 2nd Duke of Lennox and Duke of Richmond*, 1623

15 William Wissing, *Mary II when Princess of Orange*, 1685

16 Sir Peter Paul Rubens, *Self-portrait*, 1622

17 Sir Peter Lely, *Mary II, when Princess*, c.1672

18 Sir Anthony Van Dyck, *Charles I in three positions*, c.1635–6

19 Sir Peter Paul Rubens, *Portrait of a woman*, c.1628–30

20 Leonard Knyff, *A view of Windsor Castle*, c.1705

21 William Dobson, *Charles II when Prince of Wales*, 1644

22 Adriaen Hanneman, *William III when Prince of Orange*, 1664

23 Sir Anthony Van Dyck, *Queen Henrietta Maria*, c.1632

24 Simon Verelst, *Mary of Modena, Duchess of York*, c.1635

■ FURNITURE

25 English walnut and seaweed marquetry bureau attributed to Gerrit Jensen, late 17th century.

26 English Boulle marquetry cabinet, attributed to Gerrit Jensen, c.1695. Made for William III and Mary II.

27 Pair of English giltwood candle stands, c.1740. Purchased by Queen Elizabeth, consort of King George VI, in 1947. Formerly at Ditchley Park, Oxfordshire.

28 Astronomical clock by Jakob Mayr, Augsburg, late 17th century.

29 English gilt gesso chairs, c.1730 and later.

30 French ebony cabinet-on-stand, carved with scenes from contemporary literature, c.1650.

31 Ebony and giltwood centre table by Morel & Seddon, c.1828.

32 Giltwood pier table with scagliola (imitation marble) top, by Marsh & Tatham, 1814. Made for Carlton House, George IV's private residence in London when Prince of Wales.

33 English giltwood pier glass, early 19th century.

34 Pair of French marble and gilt-bronze candelabra, late 18th century.

35 French gilt-bronze mantel clock, case by R. Osmond, movement by J. Lepaute, c.1780.

36 Pair of rouge marble and gilt-bronze candelabra, late 18th century.

37 English gilt-bronze chandelier by Hancock & Rixon, 1828.

■ PORCELAIN

38 Chinese *famille rose* punch bowl, mid-18th century.

39 Pair of Chinese blue and gold porcelain vases and covers with French gilt-bronze mounts, early 18th century.

40 Chinese blue porcelain cistern with French gilt-bronze mounts, mid-18th century. Possibly belonged to Mme de Pompadour.

41 Pair of Chinese white porcelain vases, presented to Queen Victoria for her Diamond Jubilee (1897) by the Emperor of China.

Paul van Somer,
James I, c.1620

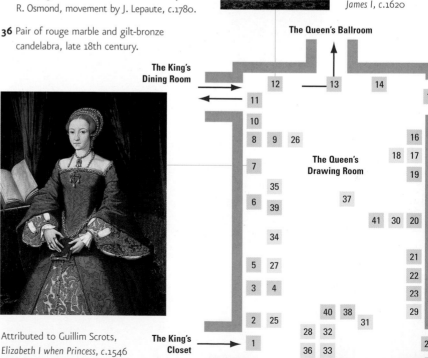

Attributed to Guillim Scrots,
Elizabeth I when Princess, c.1546

THE KING'S DINING ROOM

ROOM PLAN →

THIS ROOM RETAINS MUCH of its original Charles II character, although it is now rather dark, as it is lit only by windows looking into the Grand Staircase. The ceiling depicts a banquet of the gods and the still lifes of fruit, fish and fowl in the coving are particularly attractive. The magnificent wood carvings are by Grinling Gibbons and his assistant Henry Phillips, but were not all originally in this room; the palm fronds over the alcoves, for instance, were in the old Royal Chapel.

The room also owes something of its present appearance to Queen Mary, Consort of King George V, who in the early twentieth century oversaw the restoration of the state apartments at Windsor Castle. She replaced the oak wainscot here and installed the two Brussels tapestries with the arms of William III. Other pieces from this set of tapestries are at Het Loo, William III's palace in Holland.

THIS ROOM CONTAINS THE FIRST OF VERRIO'S SURVIVING PAINTED CEILINGS FROM THE TIME OF CHARLES II

CHARLES II DINED IN PUBLIC IN THIS ROOM ON CERTAIN DAYS, AND AFTER EATING WITHDREW TO THE KING'S DRAWING ROOM

BELOW: Details of the ceiling frieze from the King's Dining Room.

Samuel Pepys visits Windsor Castle, 26 February 1666

So took coach and to Windsor to the Garter ... to St George's Chapel. ... It is a noble place indeed, and a good Quire of voices. Great bowing by all the people, the poor Knights particularly, to the Altar. After prayers we to see the plate of the Chapel and the Robes of Knights, and a man to show us the banners of the several Knights in being, which hang up over the stalls. ... This being done, to the King's House and to observe the neatness and contrivance of the house and gates; it is the most Romantic castle that is in the world ... the prospect that is in the Balcony in the Queen's lodgings, and the Terrace and walk ... being the best in the world, sure.

PICTURES

1 Jacob Huysmans, *Catherine of Braganza*, 1664 (overmantel)

2 Sir Godfrey Kneller, *Michael Alphonsus Shen Fu-Tsung, 'The Chinese Convert'*, 1687

3 John Riley, *Bridget Holmes*, 1686

4 John Michael Wright, *John Lacy*, c.1668–70

FURNITURE

5 French ebony and Boulle marquetry secretaire, the base c.1710, the upper part c.1770, by E. Levasseur. Bought by George IV in 1812.

6 Pair of English giltwood torchères, c.1730.

7 Ebony and Boulle marquetry breakfront cabinet, early 19th century.

8 Pair of English giltwood pier glasses, c.1740.

9 French ebony and Boulle marquetry drop-front secretaire, late 18th century.

10 French Boulle marquetry pedestal clock, late 17th century, with 19th-century movement by B. L. Vulliamy. Purchased by George IV in 1820.

11 Pair of giltwood pier tables attributed to Jean Pelletier, c.1699.

12 Pair of English giltwood pier glasses with cypher of Queen Anne, early 18th century and later.

13 English walnut and floral marquetry side table, late 17th century.

14 English walnut and seaweed marquetry side table, late 17th century.

15 Six gilt-metal wall sconces with cypher of Charles II, 19th century.

16 Ebony medicine cabinet with silver-gilt mounts, Augsburg, early 17th century, on a later stand.

17 Group of caned walnut chairs, late 17th century.

18 Boulle marquetry mantel clock, late 17th century, with 19th-century movement by B. L. Vulliamy.

19 Ebony bracket clock by Thomas Tompion, late 17th century.

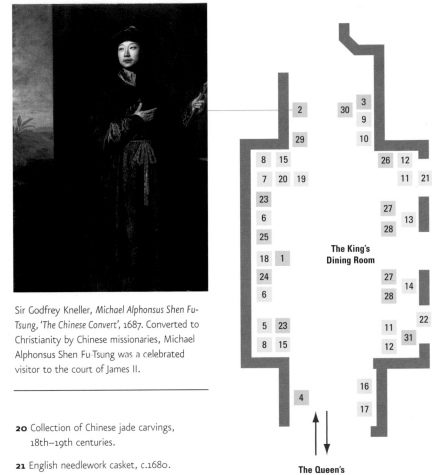

Sir Godfrey Kneller, *Michael Alphonsus Shen Fu-Tsung, 'The Chinese Convert'*, 1687. Converted to Christianity by Chinese missionaries, Michael Alphonsus Shen Fu-Tsung was a celebrated visitor to the court of James II.

20 Collection of Chinese jade carvings, 18th–19th centuries.

21 English needlework casket, c.1680.

22 English silver-mounted marquetry bellows, late 17th century. Traditionally said to have belonged to Charles II's mistress Nell Gwynn.

TAPESTRIES

23 Two Brussels panels with the arms of William III and Mary II, designed by Daniel Marot, c.1700. Purchased by Queen Mary in 1914.

PORCELAIN

24 Two pairs of Chinese porcelain *famille verte* baluster vases, 17th century.

25 Group of Japanese Arita porcelain 'Hampton Court' vases and square bottles, c.1700, some with 18th-century French gilt-bronze mounts.

26 Japanese Arita porcelain baluster vase, c.1700, with later French gilt-bronze mounts.

27 Four Chinese porcelain long-necked bottles, c.1700.

28 Pair of Japanese porcelain candelabra, late 17th century, with French gilt-bronze mounts, late 18th century.

SCULPTURE

29 Terracotta bust of Charles II, late 17th century.

30 French bronze equestrian group of Henri IV, early 19th century.

31 Italian bronze statuette of a fawn, 16th century.

The King's Dining Room

The Queen's Drawing Room

THE QUEEN'S BALLROOM

ROOM PLAN →

THE QUEEN'S BALLROOM, or gallery, is also part of the Queen's Apartment. Again it was extensively remodelled by Wyatville for William IV but retains a Charles II dado and carved cornice. Since the nineteenth century this room has also been known as the Van Dyck Room and is hung entirely with portraits by him. The silver furniture here is also exceptional – a very rare survival of the grandest seventeenth-century royal taste. Comparable examples now only exist at Knole in Kent and Rosenborg Castle in Copenhagen.

The white marble chimneypiece, one of George III's, was brought from the Queen's Bedchamber when the latter was converted into part of the Royal Library. The three magnificent glass chandeliers are among the finest examples in England.

During a state visit to Windsor Castle, the visiting head of state receives members of the Diplomatic Corps here.

Sir Anthony Van Dyck, *Thomas Killigrew and William Lord Crofts (?), 1638*

PICTURES

1 Sir Anthony Van Dyck, *Charles I in Robes of State*, 1636

2 Sir Anthony Van Dyck, *Portrait of a woman*, c.1634–5

3 Sir Anthony Van Dyck, *Thomas Killigrew and William, Lord Crofts(?)*, 1638

4 Sir Anthony Van Dyck, *George Villiers, 2nd Duke of Buckingham, and Lord Francis Villiers*, 1635

5 Sir Anthony Van Dyck, *Lady Mary Villiers, Duchess of Richmond, as St Agnes*, c.1637

6 Sir Anthony Van Dyck, *The three eldest children of Charles I*, 1635

7 Sir Anthony Van Dyck, *Beatrice of Cusance, Princess of Cantecroix and Duchess of Lorraine*, c.1635

8 Gerrit van Honthorst, *The four eldest children of the King and Queen of Bohemia*, 1641

FURNITURE

9 Pair of English Boulle marquetry writing tables by Louis Le Gaigneur. Purchased by George IV in 1815.

10 Pair of French corner cupboards with Japanese lacquer panels and gilt-bronze mounts, mid-18th century. Purchased by George IV in 1829.

11 French giltwood seat furniture by Georges Jacob, c.1785. Supplied by Dominique Daguerre for the Prince of Wales at Carlton House.

12 Two ebony cabinets with Japanese lacquer panels, one French, c.1770; the other made to match by Morel & Hughes, 1812.

13 English silver mirror, c.1670.

14 French gilt-bronze mantel clock by J.-A. Lépine, 1790. Purchased by George IV in that year. The time is indicated on the eyeballs. The base contains a small musical organ which is controlled by pulling one of the earrings.

15 English silver mirror attributed to Andrew Moore, 1699. Made for William III at Kensington Palace.

16 Pair of cabinets veneered with cocus wood and with silver mounts, c.1665. Probably made for Queen Henrietta Maria. Presented to King George V by Lord Rothschild, 1910.

17 Silver pier glass and table, c.1685, with *repoussé* relief decoration. Made for Charles II.

18 Set of three English cut-glass chandeliers, c.1800.

19 Seven silver sconces, with *repoussé* decoration of Garter badges, c.1680.

20 Two porphyry vases with gilt-bronze mounts, c.1780.

21 Pair of French Boulle marquetry torchères with gilt-bronze mounts, c.1700. Purchased by George IV in 1814.

PORCELAIN

22 Pair of porcelain tureens and covers with gilt-bronze mounts, 19th century.

The Queen's Audience Chamber

The Queen's Ballroom

The Queen's Drawing Room

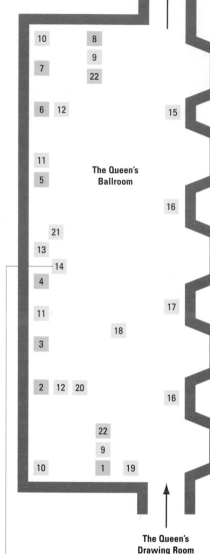

The Negress Head Clock by J-A. Lépine, 1790.

THE QUEEN'S AUDIENCE CHAMBER

ROOM PLAN →

THIS ROOM AND THE ADJOINING PRESENCE CHAMBER give an idea of the appearance of all the state apartments as remodelled for Charles II by Hugh May and his team of brilliant craftsmen. Verrio's painted ceiling shows Catherine of Braganza (wife of Charles II) being drawn in a chariot by swans towards a temple of virtue, while the cove of the ceiling is treated as a *trompe-l'oeil* balustrade. The general form of the ceiling is inspired by Le Brun's work at Versailles. The cornice, carved with acanthus leaves, and the festoons of fruit and flowers framing portraits in the overdoors are by Grinling Gibbons, Henry Phillips and their workshop. The oak wainscot, framing tapestries, recalls the original appearance of the Queen's Drawing Room (page 38), though these particular tapestries were acquired for George IV in Paris in 1825. The chimneypiece, by William Kent, was brought from St James's Palace in the early nineteenth century.

THIS ROOM IS ONE OF THE BEST-PRESERVED OF CHARLES II'S INTERIORS AT WINDSOR

ORIGINALLY THE QUEEN'S CHAIR OF STATE STOOD IN THIS ROOM

BELOW: THE QUEEN'S AUDIENCE CHAMBER. Though inspired by Louis XIV's palace interiors, the use of wainscot and wood carvings rather than marble gives the rooms at Windsor a different character.

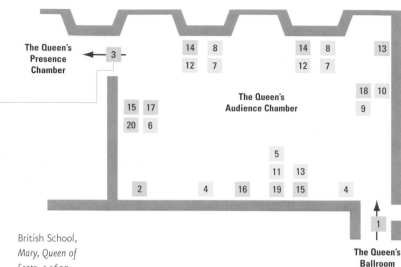

British School,
*Mary, Queen of
Scots, c.1620*

PICTURES

Over doors

1 Gerrit van Honthorst, *William II, Prince of
Orange, c.1640*

2 Gerrit van Honthorst, *Frederick Henry, Prince
of Orange, 1631*

3 British School, *Mary, Queen of Scots, c.1620*

FURNITURE

4 Two Chinese lacquer cabinets, late 17th
century, on English giltwood tables, c.1740.

5 Giltwood firescreen with Beauvais tapestry
panel by Michel Vellaud, 1815.

6 Flemish ebony cabinet-on-stand with gilt-
bronze mounts, late 17th century and later.

7 Pair of English giltwood pier tables, c.1760.
Purchased by Queen Mary in 1932.
Formerly at Chesterfield House.

8 Pair of English giltwood pier glasses, early
19th century.

9 Ebony cabinet with *pietra dura* (hardstone)
panels of flowers and dwarfs, by A.-L.
Bellangé, c.1820. Purchased by George IV
in 1825.

10 English gilt gesso chairs, c.1730 and later.

11 Patinated and gilt-bronze mantel clock
with palm tree and figures, by Justin
Vulliamy, late 18th century.

12 Pair of bronze lamps by Vulliamy, 1811.
Purchased by George IV for Carlton House.

13 Pair of English giltwood x-frame armchairs
attributed to Henry Williams, 1737.

PORCELAIN

14 Two pairs of Japanese Imari porcelain vases
and covers, late 17th century.

15 Two pairs of large Chinese blue and white
vases and covers, c.1700.

16 Pair of French white porcelain and gilt-
bronze candelabra, late 18th century.

17 Garniture of three Delft pottery vases and
covers, c.1700.

TAPESTRIES

Three Gobelins panels from *The History of Esther*
after J.-F. de Troy, woven by Audran and
Cozette, 1779–87, purchased by George IV in
1825.

18 The Coronation of Esther

19 The Triumph of Mordecai

20 The Toilet of Esther

Antonio Verrio's ceiling for the Queen's Audience Chamber (detail).

THE QUEEN'S PRESENCE CHAMBER

ROOM PLAN →

THIS ROOM IS USED BY THE KNIGHTS OF THE GARTER AS THEIR ROBING ROOM BEFORE THE PROCESSION TO ST GEORGE'S CHAPEL ON GARTER DAY

VERRIO'S CEILING IN THIS ROOM SHOWS (appropriately) Catherine of Braganza seated under a canopy held by zephyrs while figures of Envy and Sedition retreat before the outstretched Sword of Justice. The cornice and carved festoons of the overmantel and over doors are further demonstrations of the genius of the English seventeenth-century school of wood carvers.

The large marble chimneypiece incorporates a clock flanked by reclining figures of Vigilance and Patience, and was carved by John Bacon R.A. in 1789 for Queen Charlotte's Saloon at Buckingham House. The Gobelins tapestries were acquired by George IV.

**The Queen's
Guard Chamber**

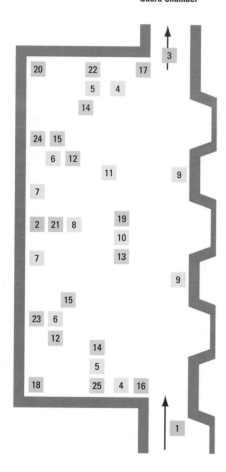

**The Queen's
Audience Chamber**

■ PICTURES

Over door

1 After Sir Peter Lely, *Frances Stuart, Duchess of Richmond and Lennox*, c.1678–80

Overmantel

2 After Pierre Mignard, *Elizabeth Charlotte, Princess Palatine, Duchess of Orleans, with her son, Philip, and her daughter, Elizabeth*, c.1660

Over door

3 Edmund Lily, *William, Duke of Gloucester*, 1698

■ FURNITURE

4 Eight Roman giltwood armchairs with embroidered velvet covers, early 18th century. Purchased by George IV in 1827.

5 Pair of Boulle and lacquer cabinets, 18th and 19th centuries.

6 Pair of English giltwood pier tables, c.1760, purchased by Queen Mary from Chesterfield House in 1932, and probably originally from Stowe in Buckinghamshire.

7 Two English gilt gesso candle stands, early 18th century.

8 Giltwood firescreen with Beauvais tapestry panel, late 18th century.

9 Pair of English giltwood pier glasses, early 19th century.

10 English rosewood and brass inlaid library table, c.1820.

11 Persian wool carpet, late 19th century.

■ PORCELAIN

12 Pair of celadon porcelain candelabra with gilt-bronze mounts by the Vulliamys, 1819.

13 Chinese celadon porcelain dish, 14th century, with French gilt-bronze mounts, c.1730.

14 Pair of celadon porcelain ewers with French gilt-bronze mounts, 18th century.

15 Four Chinese celadon vases with French gilt-bronze mounts, late 18th–early 19th century.

■ SCULPTURE

16 White marble bust of Ferdinand, Duke of Brunswick, late 18th century.

17 White marble bust of John, Lord Ligonier, by L. F. Roubiliac, c.1750.

18 White marble bust of the duc de Villars, by A. Coysevox, 1718.

19 Two French bronze groups of the *Rape of the Sabines*, after Giambologna, 18th century.

20 White marble bust of Maréchal Vauban, by A. Coysevox, 1706.

21 White marble clock case designed by Robert Adam and carved by John Bacon the Elder, 1789. Movement by B. L. Vulliamy.

■ TAPESTRIES

Four Gobelins panels from *The History of Esther* after J.-F. de Troy, woven by Audran and Cozette, 1779–87.

22 The Banquet of Esther

23 The Disdain of Mordecai

24 Esther supplicates for the lives of her people

25 The Judgement of Haman

THE QUEEN'S GUARD CHAMBER

ROOM PLAN →

ABOVE: THE QUEEN'S GUARD CHAMBER, photographed by Disderi in 1867 (detail). Disderi's photographs were an invaluable resource when restoration work began on areas damaged by the fire of 1992, such as the Crimson Drawing Room (page 63).

ORIGINALLY THERE WERE TWO GUARD CHAMBERS at Windsor, one at the entry to the King's Apartment (on the site of the Grand Reception Room) and this, which was the entrance to the Queen's Apartment. It was remodelled in the Gothic style with a plaster rib vault by Wyatville for George IV. Wyatville also added the large bay window over the State Entrance, which gives good views into the Quadrangle. Immediately opposite is the George IV Gateway, beyond which the Long Walk continues for three miles into Windsor Great Park.

A unique feature of the room are the French flags hanging over the busts of the Dukes of Marlborough and Wellington, the Bourbon fleurs-de-lys for Marlborough and the Republican tricolour for Wellington. These are presented each year to the Sovereign as quit-rents for the estates at Blenheim and Stratfield Saye respectively. The chimneypiece is of polished limestone.

The display of arms on the walls of this appropriately martial room derives from Sir Samuel Rush Meyrick's arrangement, which in turn was based on seventeenth-century ideas for the decorative use of arms in the Royal Armouries. The Indian ivory throne in the centre of the Guard Chamber was a present from the Maharajah of Travancore to Queen Victoria in 1851. Today this room is used for receptions of the Diplomatic Corps when they come to pay their respects to a visiting head of state and the heralds change into their tabards here before the Garter Service in St George's Chapel.

■ PICTURES

1 Joachim Kayser and Johannes Anton von Klyher, *Frederick, Prince of Wales*, on horseback, 1727 (overmantel)

2 Spanish School, *Portrait of a Spanish nobleman*, 16th century

■ FURNITURE

3 Coronation thrones of Jacobean design made by Morris & Co. for King George V and Queen Mary and copied from a chair at Knole. Used in the second part of the Coronation, 22 June 1911.

4 Throne with the arms of The Duke of Edinburgh. Made by Beresford & Hicks.

5 Oak thrones of King George V, Queen Mary and Edward, Prince of Wales. Made by Morris & Co. for the Investiture of the Prince of Wales in 1911.

6 Coronation thrones made by Howard & Sons for King George V and Queen Mary and copied from a chair at Knole. Used in the first part of the Coronation, 22 June 1911.

7 The Waterloo Elm armchair. Made by Thomas Chippendale the Younger from part of an elm growing on the field of Waterloo. Presented to George IV in 1821.

8 Gilt-bronze chandelier by W. and G. Perry, 1828.

9 Indian ivory chair of state and footstool. Presented to Queen Victoria in 1851 by the Maharajah of Travancore and shown at the Great Exhibition of the same year.

■ ARMS & ARMOUR

10 Guidon of The Queen's Royal Irish Hussars. (A guidon is the name given to the flag of a light cavalry regiment.)

11 Colour of the Sovereign's Company of the Grenadier Guards.

12 Trophies of firearms, armour and edged weapons, English, 18th–19th centuries.

13 Range of display cabinets containing European armour, firearms and edged weapons. Mainly from the collection of George IV at Carlton House.

A Case containing a 17th-century Italian child's half-armour and a display of 18th- and 19th-century small swords, an embossed and damascened shield attributed to Eliseus Libaerts, c.1562-3, and Henry VIII's hunting sword, made by Diego de Çaias, 1544, and acquired by HM The Queen in 1966.

B Case containing swords and daggers, including a dress sword with a mid-17th-century Dutch carved ivory hilt.

C Case containing pistols, including several Scottish flintlock Highland pistols (known as 'tacks'), 1780–1800; and a pair of flintlock pistols by Diemar, c.1780, with inlaid relief decoration to the stocks.

D Case including a half-armour presented to Charles I when Prince of Wales by Charles Emanuel of Savoy.

14 Japanese Samurai short sword, c.1420. Surrendered by Field Marshal Count Terauchi to the Supreme Allied Commander, South-East Asia (Lord Louis Mountbatten) to mark the end of the War in the Far East, 1945.

■ SCULPTURE

15 Bronze bust of Philip II King of Spain, by Leone Leoni, mid-16th century. Purchased by George IV in 1825.

16 Patinated lead equestrian group of William Augustus, Duke of Cumberland, attributed to Henry Cheere, mid-18th century.

17 Bronze bust of the Emperor Charles V by Leone Leoni, mid-16th century. Purchased by George IV in 1825.

18 Bronze bust of Ferdinand, Duke of Alba, by Leone Leoni, mid-16th century. Purchased by George IV in 1825.

19 Bronze bust of Enea Caprara by Massimiliano Soldani-Benzi, c.1695.

20 White marble bust of Sir Winston Churchill by Oscar Nemon, 1956. Commissioned by HM The Queen.

21 White marble bust of John Churchill, 1st Duke of Marlborough, by John Henning, early 19th century. Beneath the annual rent banner for Blenheim Palace.

22 White marble bust of Arthur, 1st Duke of Wellington, by Sir Francis Chantrey, 1835. Beneath the annual rent banner for Stratfield Saye House.

23 Bronze bust of Lord Nelson by Mrs Anne Seymour Damer, 1828.

■ METALWORK

24 Silver-plated 19th-century replica of the silver-gilt 'Shield of Achilles', designed by John Flaxman in 1821.

25 Silver, gold and enamel shield designed by P. von Cornelius, 1842. A christening present to King Edward VII from King Frederick William IV of Prussia.

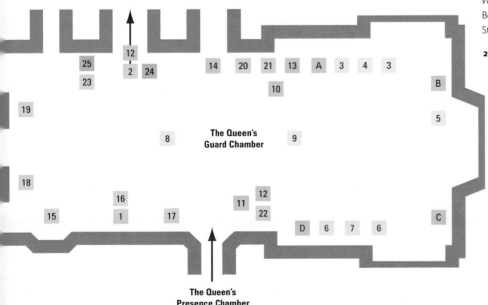

St George's Hall

ROOM PLAN →

ST GEORGE'S HALL IS ONE OF THE MOST HISTORIC ROOMS in the castle. For six centuries it has been associated with the Order of the Garter.

It occupies the site of Edward III's Great Hall and Chapel. These had been redecorated by Hugh May for Charles II, with murals by Verrio and carvings by Grinling Gibbons, and formed the climax of baroque Windsor. The murals were very largely destroyed, except for a few areas which survived beneath the later plaster, when Wyatville knocked together the old hall and chapel in 1829 to create this enormous room. One fragment of the ceiling, showing Charles II, has recently been reacquired for the Royal Collection (see page 13).

The romantic Gothic interior was inspired by Sir Walter Scott, whose novels were greatly admired by George IV. When the interior of the castle was remodelled in the 1820s by Wyatville, Gothic was chosen for all the processional

ST GEORGE'S HALL IS OVER 55 METRES (180 FEET) LONG

THE NEW OAK ROOF IS THE LARGEST OF ITS TYPE TO HAVE BEEN BUILT IN THE TWENTIETH CENTURY

THE HALL IS THE SETTING FOR STATE BANQUETS HELD BY THE QUEEN

ABOVE: The state banquet held by The Queen in St George's Hall, Windsor Castle, for Queen Margrethe and Prince Henrik of Denmark as part of their State Visit in February 2000.

LEFT: Joseph Nash, *Queen Victoria and Louis-Philippe entering St George's Hall for the Garter Banquet, 11 October 1844*

OPPOSITE: St George's Hall after the restoration of 1992–97.

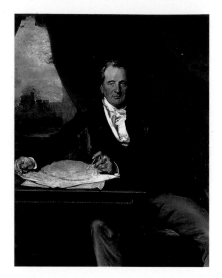

Sir Thomas Lawrence, *Sir Jeffry Wyatville*, 1830.

spaces while an eclectic classical style was mainly used for the reception rooms. In St George's Hall, Wyatville's ceiling (of plaster grained to resemble oak) was decorated with the coats of arms of all the Knights of the Garter from their foundation, a scheme devised by Thomas Willement, George IV's heraldic artist. The walls were then further embellished with alternate trophies of weapons and figures in armour.

St George's Hall was seriously damaged by the fire of 1992. The ceiling and the east wall, which contained a large double-sided organ by Father Willis, were destroyed. The new green oak roof, designed by Giles Downes of the Sidell Gibson Partnership, is of stepped arched trussed construction. It is considerably more steeply pitched than was Wyatville's, and the overall proportions and appearance of the room have thus been greatly improved. The new oak screen at the east end, also designed by Giles Downes, supports oak carvings of the Queen's Beasts on the parapet, which were given by the City of London.

The decorative plaster Garter and rose in the gable was presented by the Commonwealth; each of the fifty-four petals represents a country. The replacement oak floor incorporates trees grown on the estates of Knights of the Garter, and the shields of every Garter Knight have been re-created on the ceiling and continued round the room. Overall, it is a vigorous example of heraldic decoration and is completed by the heraldic stained glass, created by John Reyntiens, in the top lights of the windows. The full-length portraits and the marble busts form a royal pantheon, while Wyatville's great Gothic 'throne of Edward III' has been reinstated in its old position at the east end.

The King's Champion

The figure of the King's Champion faces down St George's Hall from the new balcony at the east end. The Champion, an hereditary office held by the Dymoke family, used to ride into the coronation banquet held for a new monarch in Westminster Hall, throw down his gauntlet three times and challenge anyone to deny the authority of the new sovereign. The ceremony last took place at George IV's Coronation in 1821.

The figure wears a suit of armour made at Greenwich in 1585 for Sir Christopher Hatton, and given by him to Robert Dudley, Earl of Leicester, the favourite of Elizabeth I. The armour is supposed to have been worn by a member of the Dymoke family in the role of King's Champion at the Coronations of both George I and George II. It was presented to King Edward VII in 1901.

The Lantern Lobby

▪ PICTURES

1 Sir Anthony Van Dyck, *James I*, c.1635–6

2 Daniel Mytens, *Charles I*, 1631

3 Sir Peter Lely and a later hand, *Charles II*, c.1672

4 Sir Peter Lely and studio, *James II*, c.1665–70

5 Sir Godfrey Kneller, *Mary II*, 1690

6 Sir Godfrey Kneller, *William III*, c.1690

7 Studio of Sir Godfrey Kneller, *Queen Anne*, c.1705

8 Studio of Sir Godfrey Kneller, *George I*, c.1715

9 Enoch Seeman, *George II*, c.1730

10 Gainsborough Dupont, *George III*, c.1794

11 Sir Thomas Lawrence, *George IV*, c.1825

▪ SCULPTURE

Twenty-one marble busts of sovereigns and other royal members of the Order of the Garter:

North Wall

12 J. M. Rysbrack, *Queen Anne*, c.1710

13 Joseph Nollekens, *Frederick, Duke of York*, 1813

14 Peter Turnerelli, *George III*, 1810

15 Sir Francis Chantrey, *George IV*, 1826

16 Sir Francis Chantrey, *William IV*, 1837

17 Edward Onslow Ford, *Queen Victoria*, 1898

18 R. W. Sievier, *Albert, Prince Consort*, 1842

19 Sidney March, *Edward VII*, 1902

20 J. E. Boehm, *Alfred, Duke of Edinburgh*, 1879

21 F. J. Williamson, *Leopold, Duke of Albany*, 1883

22 F. J. Williamson, *Arthur, Duke of Connaught*, 1885

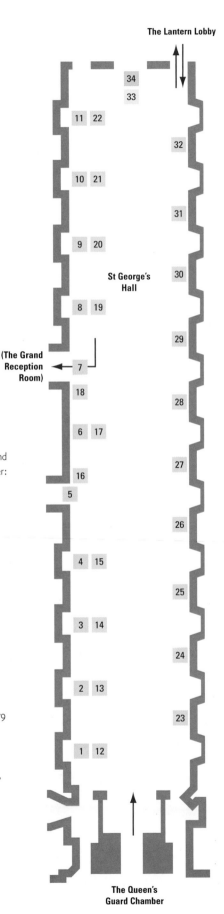

St George's Hall

(The Grand Reception Room)

The Queen's Guard Chamber

South Wall

23 J. M. Rysbrack, *Frederick, Prince of Wales*, c.1750

24 Joseph Nollekens, *William, Duke of Cumberland*, 1814 (copy of a bust by Rysbrack of 1754)

25 Joseph Nollekens, *Edward, Duke of York*, c.1766

26 J. C. Lochee, *Frederick, Duke of York*, c.1787

27 William Behnes, *Ernest, Duke of Cumberland*, 1826

28 William Behnes, *Edward, Duke of Kent*, 1828

29 William Theed, *Augustus Frederick, Duke of Sussex* (posthumous bust), 1881

30 Lawrence Macdonald, *Adolphus, Duke of Cambridge*, 1848

31 G. G. Adams, *George, Duke of Cambridge*, 1888

32 W. White after R. Begas, *Frederick III, King of Prussia*, 1897

▪ FURNITURE

33 Massive carved oak chair of state known as 'Edward III's throne', c.1835

▪ ARMOUR

34 The armour of the King's Champion. Made at Greenwich in 1585 for Sir Christopher Hatton, and given by him to Robert Dudley, Earl of Leicester. Presented to Edward VII in 1901.

N ←

THE LANTERN LOBBY

THE FIRE OF NOVEMBER 1992
BEGAN HERE

AMONG OTHER TREASURES, THE
ROOM NOW CONTAINS A SUPERB SUIT
OF ARMOUR WHICH BELONGED TO
HENRY VIII

RIGHT: The Lantern.
BELOW: Henry VIII's armour, c.1540.

THIS NEW ROOM, WHICH OCCUPIES THE SITE of Queen Victoria's private chapel, creates a new processional sequence through the castle. The private chapel was completely destroyed in the fire of 1992. Part of the carved stone reredos above the altar survived the flames and has been restored as a memorial to the conflagration. The inscription reads: 'The fire of 20th November 1992 began here. Restoration of the fire-damaged area was completed five years later, on 20th November 1997, the fiftieth anniversary of the wedding of Her Majesty Queen Elizabeth II and His Royal Highness The Duke of Edinburgh.'

The new, tall, octagonal lobby created in the gutted area was inspired by Ely Cathedral and by the Abbey of Batalha in Portugal. The result was a carefully proportioned space which neatly solved the problem of the change of axis in the north-east corner of the castle between St George's Hall and the royal apartments to the south and east. Eight oak columns support a ribbed vault of laminated oak and a central glazed lantern. Though the feel is medieval, the

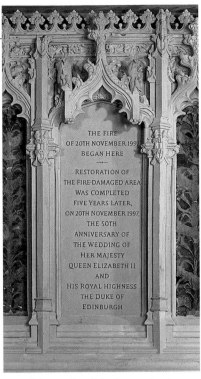

finely executed and original detail celebrates modern Gothic design and British craftsmanship, especially in the joinery of the columns and vault, and in such features as the stamped red leather and delicate ironwork of the central doors to St George's Hall. There is also a finely inlaid floor of English marbles depicting the Garter Star.

The Lobby has been partly conceived as a treasury, with wall cases to display objects in silver-gilt from the Royal Collection, including chapel and buffet plate and some of George IV's more unusual commissions such as Flaxman's National Cup (1824). It also contains Henry VIII's armour, a masterpiece from the workshop established by the King at Greenwich.

Part of the reredos of the former chapel, incorporating the inscribed tablet.

ARMOUR

1 Suit of armour made at Greenwich for Henry VIII, c.1540

DISPLAY CASES

2 Buffet of silver-gilt vessels and dishes, 17th–19th centuries, including a centrepiece designed by William Kent and made for Frederick, Prince of Wales, by George Wickes, 1745; and a pair of Charles II firedogs adapted for George IV and engraved with his arms.

3 Selection of standing cups, 16th–19th centuries, including two German cups with nautilus shells, one by Nicolaus Schmidt, c.1600; an ivory cup from the collection of William Beckford; a 16th-century mother-of-pearl casket and a 17th-century amber casket; a partly gilt equestrian statuette of Gustavus Adolphus, Augsburg, early 17th century; the National Cup, designed by John Flaxman, 1824; and the Dürer Cup, designed by A. W. N. Pugin (based on a design by Albrecht Dürer), 1826–7 (the last two supplied by the firm of Rundell, Bridge & Rundell).

4 Selection from the private chapel plate of Windsor Castle, Buckingham Palace and Brighton Pavilion. English, 17th–19th centuries.

PICTURE

5 George Weymouth, *Prince Philip, Duke of Edinburgh*, 1995

SCULPTURE

6 Bronze bust of Her Majesty The Queen by the Australian artist John Dowie, 1987

The inlaid marble centre to the floor of the Lantern Lobby shows the Order of the Garter.

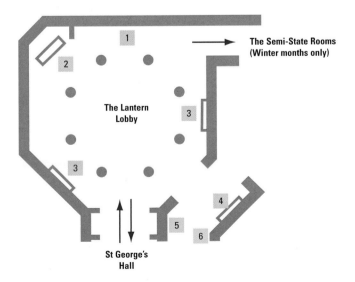

The Semi-State Rooms

The Semi-State Rooms were created by George IV in the 1820s as part of a new series of royal apartments for his personal occupation. Designed by Wyatville, they were decorated and furnished by Morel & Seddon. They continue in use by The Queen for official entertaining and are therefore only open to the public during the winter months. Damaged in the 1992 fire, they have been restored to their original appearance and contain furniture and works of art chosen or commissioned by George IV. They are reached via the New Corridor.

ABOVE: Laurits Regner Tuxen, *The Family of Queen Victoria in 1887* (detail), painted in the Green Drawing Room.

RIGHT: Part of the Sèvres porcelain service made for Louis XVI, which is on display in the Green Drawing Room.

THE NEW CORRIDOR

TWO PORTRAITS HANG HERE, attributed to Allan Ramsay, *Elizabeth Albertina, Princess of Mecklenburg-Strelitz, c.1760* and Sir Joshua Reynolds, *George III, c.1780.*

THE GREEN DRAWING ROOM
(Viewed from the Crimson Drawing Room, through the doors to the right.)

THE GREEN DRAWING ROOM largely survived the fire but was saturated by water. The opportunity was taken to replace the silk for the walls and redesign the window curtains to match more closely the Morel & Seddon scheme designed for George IV, who had intended this room as a library. After the establishment of the new Royal Library on the north side of the castle, the bookcases were adapted to display another of his acquisitions, the Sèvres service made for Louis XVI, which is one of the finest in existence.

The gilded ceiling of this room is Wyatville's most accomplished ceiling at Windsor. There is a tautness and perfection of detail in the work executed during George IV's lifetime that is lacking from the state rooms decorated in the next reign. The seat furniture is part of a huge set commissioned by George IV from Morel & Seddon, and the bronzes were also mainly assembled by George IV and include four groups of *The Four Seasons*, mounted as candelabra by Caffieri for the comte d'Orsay. The Axminster carpet was designed by Ludwig Gruner for Queen Victoria and shown at the Great Exhibition in 1851, where it was greatly admired as an excellent example of English manufacture. It survived the fire of 1992 but is now too delicate to allow visitors to walk on it.

THE CRIMSON DRAWING ROOM

ROOM PLAN →

LIKE THE GREEN DRAWING ROOM, the Crimson Drawing Room is very much an expression of George IV's personal taste. The general form of the room – a long rectangle with a broad bay window overlooking the East Terrace garden – was designed by Jeffry Wyatville, but the decoration was entrusted to Morel & Seddon. They were responsible for the wall decorations, including the framed panels of silk, and the window curtains. The room also incorporates fittings from George IV's earlier London residence, Carlton House, notably the black marble and bronze chimneypiece by the Vulliamys (a pair to that in the Green Drawing Room) and the four pairs of carved and gilded doors.

During the 1992 fire the ceiling of the Crimson Drawing Room collapsed, and large areas of the walls were damaged by heat. The restoration was carried out by Donald Insall and Partners, a firm of specialist conservation architects responsible for all the restoration, as opposed to the new work, in the fire-damaged part of the castle. The fire created an opportunity to reweave the silk

THE CRIMSON DRAWING ROOM WAS THE PRINCIPAL INTERIOR IN GEORGE IV'S SEMI-STATE ROOMS

THE REINSTATED CEILING INCORPORATES MANY FRAGMENTS OF THE ORIGINAL PLASTERWORK BY BERNASCONI, SALVAGED FROM THE DEBRIS AFTER THE 1992 FIRE

BELOW: The Crimson Drawing Room, photographed by Disderi in 1867.

damask wall hangings to the striped pattern and rich crimson colour chosen for the room by George IV. Window curtains of the same material were also reinstated to designs which reflect the lavishness of Morel & Seddon's original scheme, using photographs of the room taken in 1867. The new curtains and rich *passementerie* were devised by Pamela Lewis, who was responsible for the design of all the upholstery restoration.

As intended by George IV, the room is furnished with Morel & Seddon's seat furniture, and with sumptuous French works of art including three pairs of *pietra dura* and ebony cabinets and six ormolu candelabra by Thomire. The vast crystal chandelier, though made for George IV, was hung here in the early twentieth century by Queen Mary. It was severely damaged in the fire but has now been completely restored. The overall *mise-en-scène* evokes to a remarkable degree the splendour of Carlton House, George IV's London residence when he was Prince of Wales. This and the adjoining rooms are the finest and most complete examples in existence of late Georgian taste in decoration, and the restoration after the fire has enhanced their quality as a sequence of inter-related spaces.

Sir Gerald Kelly, *State Portraits of Queen Elizabeth, Queen Consort of King George VI and King George VI*, 1942–5

PICTURES

1 Sir William Beechey, *Princess Augusta*, 1795–7

2 Sir William Beechey, *Princess Mary*, 1795–7

3 Sir Gerald Kelly, *King George VI*, 1942–5

4 Sir William Beechey, *Princess Sophia*, 1795–7

5 Sir William Beechey, *Princess Amelia*, 1795–7

6 Sir Gerald Kelly, *Queen Elizabeth, Queen Consort of King George VI*, 1942–5

7 Sir William Beechey, *Princess Elizabeth*, 1795–7

8 Sir William Beechey, *Charlotte, Princess Royal*, c.1795–7

9 John Hoppner, *Edward, Duke of Kent*, c.1800

10 After John Hoppner, *George IV when Prince of Wales*, c.1800

CHIMNEYPIECE

Polished black marble, patinated and gilt-bronze, with figures of satyrs to either side. Supplied by the Vulliamys in 1807–12 for the Crimson Drawing Room at Carlton House.

The State Dining Room

[Room plan diagram showing the Crimson Drawing Room with numbered items: 16, 2, 1, 23, 23, 16, 24, 10, 3, 17, 11, 12, 4, 14, 21, 15, 19, 5, 20, 11, 12, 6, 9, 25, 17, 22, 22, 18, 13, 18, 7, 8. Arrow marked "The New Corridor" points in. "The Green Drawing Room" at bottom.]

FURNITURE

Pieces from a set of upholstered, carved and gilt beechwood seat furniture by Morel & Seddon, c.1828.

11 Two rectangular sofa tables with inlaid amboyna tops and gilt-bronze mounts, by Morel & Seddon, c.1828.

12 Two circular tables with gilt-bronze mounts, by Morel & Seddon, c.1829.

13 Six tall French Empire gilt-bronze candelabra (two of eleven lights, four of fourteen) of antique form, by Pierre-Philippe Thomire. From the Throne Room and Old Throne Room at Carlton House. Purchased by George IV in 1814.

14 Pair of French Empire seven-light lapis lazuli and gilt-bronze candelabra by Pierre-Philippe Thomire. Purchased by George IV in 1817.

15 French Empire gilt-bronze clock representing the Spirit of the Arts and inscribed *Artium Genio*, by Pierre-Philippe Thomire. Bought by George IV in 1813. From the Throne Room at Carlton House.

16 Pair of French ebony cabinets with gilt-bronze mounts and *pietra dura* panels, 1803. Acquired from M.-E. Lignereux for George IV by Sir Harry Featherstonhaugh.

17 Pair of English ebony and *pietra dura* cabinets attributed to Robert Hume, c.1820. Purchased for George IV in 1825.

18 Smaller pair of ebony, Boulle and *pietra dura* cabinets attributed to Robert Hume, c.1820.

19 An English carved and gilt beechwood pedestal supported by three winged griffins, attributed to Tatham, Bailey & Sanders, c.1811.

20 Large cut-glass and gilt-bronze 28-light chandelier, c.1810.

PORCELAIN

21 Large Chinese dark-blue porcelain vase mounted as a tripod. The gilt-bronze mounts are attributed to Thomire, c.1790.

Sir William Beechey, *Princess Elizabeth*, 1795–7

22 Pair of tall late 18th-century Sèvres porcelain vases with gilt-bronze mounts.

23 Pair of tall dark-blue Sèvres porcelain covered vases (*vase bachelier*), c.1767–70.

SCULPTURE

24 Bronze figure of *Mars* attributed to Sebastian Slodtz, early 18th century.

25 Bronze figure of *Julius Caesar* by Nicolas Coustou, early 18th century.

THE STATE DINING ROOM

IN CONTRAST TO THE GREEN AND CRIMSON DRAWING ROOMS, George IV chose the Gothic style for this room. The juxtaposition of Gothic and classical decoration was an aspect of George IV's taste also found at Carlton House.

The room was gutted in the 1992 fire, as it had been (though less badly) on a previous occasion in 1853. The largest of the sideboards, being too big to move, was destroyed, as was Beechey's painting hanging above it, *George III at a review.* The sideboard was subsequently remade to the original design.

The room has been restored to Wyatville's design with its cambered, cusped and coffered ceiling, all painted stone colour and gold. The opportunity was also taken to restore important original details removed in the twentieth century in an attempt to lighten the room. These included the pilaster strips on the walls, vigorously

BELOW: The State Dining Room. The table is laid for lunch on Gold Cup Day during Ascot Week.

modelled with gilded vines and grapes. The crimson curtains and crimson Gothic carpet reflect the original Morel & Seddon scheme, again re-created using photographs taken in 1867. The sideboards and side tables were all designed in 1827 for Morel & Seddon by A.C. Pugin with the assistance of his 15-year-old son, A. W. N. Pugin, whose first work this was. As a famous architect and designer he later disowned this juvenilia, though admitting that 'the parts were correct and exceedingly well executed'. The large St Petersburg porcelain vase was placed in the north window after the fire. It shows two of the Imperial palaces and was a gift from Tsar Nicholas I to Queen Victoria. The bronze lamps round the room were made in 1810 by the Vulliamys for Carlton House, while the huge group portrait over the sideboard is *The Family of Frederick, Prince of Wales* by George Knapton.

Benjamin Constant's 1899 portrait of Queen Victoria over the chimneypiece of the State Dining Room.

■ PICTURES

1 George Knapton, *The Family of Frederick, Prince of Wales*, 1751. The recently widowed Augusta, Princess of Wales, poses with her children in front of a portrait of the deceased Prince Frederick. Their home, the White House at Kew, is also depicted. The future King George III is second from the left.

2 Benjamin Constant, *Queen Victoria*, 1899

■ FURNITURE

Suite of Gothic revival rosewood and partly gilt dining-room furniture (dining table, sideboards, wine coolers and serving tables) with gilt-bronze mounts by Morel & Seddon from designs by A.C. and A. W. N. Pugin, 1828. The very large sideboard beneath the Knapton portrait is a

modern replica by N. E. J. Stevenson of the original, which was destroyed in the 1992 fire.

3 Gilt beechwood dining chairs originally supplied for Carlton House by Tatham & Bailey, 1815.

4 Eight patinated bronze lamps by the Vulliamys, 1811, on modern scagliola (imitation marble) pedestals.

5 French mantel clock with Sèvres porcelain panels depicting the history of timekeeping, presented to Queen Victoria by King Louis-Philippe at Windsor Castle in 1844.

6 Pair of patinated bronze candelabra with figures of the infant Hercules and the serpent, by the Vulliamys, c.1810.

■ PORCELAIN

7 Massive Russian porcelain vase with gilt-bronze handles and mounts, painted with views of Peterhof and Tsarskoe Selo. Presented to Queen Victoria by Tsar Nicholas I in 1844.

George Knapton, *The Family of Frederick, Prince of Wales*, 1751

THE OCTAGON DINING ROOM

■ FURNITURE

1 Set of Gothic revival stools, made of oak and pollard oak by Morel & Seddon, 1827-8, from designs by A. W. N. Pugin.

2 Three Gothic revival oak side tables, veneered in pollard oak, by Morel & Seddon, c.1828.

3 Set of Gothic revival oak chairs with arcaded backs, mid-19th century.

4 Oak extending dining table by Johnstone Norman & Co., 1891.

■ CLOCK

5 French patinated and gilt-bronze mantel clock by Manière, with figures emblematic of Time and Study, early 19th century.

■ CHANDELIER

6 Gilt-bronze Gothic revival chandelier, the design attributed to A. W. N. Pugin, and made by Hancock & Rixon, c.1828.

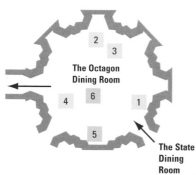

The China Corridor

This narrow passage was added by Wyatville outside the medieval curtain wall. The Gothic cases formerly housed George IV's armour collection, now shown in the Grand Vestibule and Queen's Guard Chamber. Queen Mary adapted them for the display of porcelain.

RIGHT: The Octagon Dining Room.

THE BRUNSWICK TOWER, in which this room is situated, was an addition by Wyatville. There was no medieval precedent for an octagonal tower here. It is the most satisfying of Wyatville's smaller Gothic rooms, but it too was gutted in 1992 when it became a huge chimney for the smoke and flames in the last and most dramatic episode of the fire. All the floors collapsed and the flames shot 15 metres (50 feet) into the sky above the battlements.

Despite the severity of the blaze, Wyatville's dark marble Gothic chimneypiece and the stone tracery of the windows survived. Fortunately at the time of the fire the original furnishings were in store. The room has therefore been reinstated according to Wyatville's plans. The Gothic oak furniture, designed by the young Pugin in 1827, was made by Morel & Seddon. The magnificent gilt-metal Gothic chandelier, also probably by Pugin, was found buried under 3 metres (10 feet) of rubble in the private chapel. It was restored and replaced here in the room for which it was made.

THE GRAND RECEPTION ROOM

ROOM PLAN ➤

THE GRAND RECEPTION ROOM was designed under George IV's immediate supervision with the assistance of Sir Charles Long, who bought eighteenth-century French panelling in Paris in 1825 specially for the wall decorations. This was installed with additions in composition by Francis Bernasconi, in order to frame six Gobelins tapestries from the *Jason* series, which were also bought in Paris by Sir Charles Long. Bernasconi modelled the elaborate plaster cove and ceiling, which were severely damaged in the 1992 fire but then painstakingly restored. The gilded ornaments were designed by Frederick and John Crace, who previously worked for George IV at Brighton Pavilion.

Wyatville himself was rather ambivalent about all this gilded splendour. His assistant Henry Ashton later remarked that 'the introduction of French boiserie … would never have appeared in the castle had the architect been solely guided by his own judgement'. The impressive 'Louis Quatorze' decoration was, however, a great success, starting a fashion in great English houses that lasted throughout the nineteenth century.

The three superb gilt-bronze and glass chandeliers in this room collapsed in the fire but were meticulously pieced together and restored. The parquetry floor round the edge of the room is original; blocks singed in the fire have simply been reversed. The huge malachite urn in the window is one of the largest outside Russia, and was given to Queen Victoria by Tsar Nicholas I. It was too heavy to move, but survived the fire with only superficial damage.

The room was intended by George IV as a ballroom and is now used by The Queen to greet her guests before state banquets and receptions.

THIS ROOM, PERHAPS MORE THAN ANY OTHER OF THE STATE ROOMS AT WINDSOR, REPRESENTS GEORGE IV'S PERSONAL, FRANCOPHILE TASTE

AS PART OF THE POST-1992 RESTORATION ALL THE GILDING WAS RENEWED, AND THE ROOM CAN NOW BE SEEN IN ITS ORIGINAL DAZZLING SPLENDOUR

RIGHT: The massive Russian malachite urn from the Grand Reception Room at Windsor Castle.

TAPESTRIES

Six episodes from *The Story of Jason*, woven at the Gobelins factory in Paris between 1776 and 1779, by Cozette and Audran, after paintings by Jean-François de Troy. Purchased in Paris for George IV in 1825. *(The numbers in brackets place the episodes in the order of the legend.)*

1 Jason, unfaithful to Medea, marries Glauce, daughter of King Creon of Thebes (4)

2 Soldiers sprung from the dragon's teeth turn their weapons against each other (2)

3 Medea stabs her two sons by Jason, sets fire to Corinth and departs for Athens (6)

4 Jason pledges his faith to Medea, who promises to help him with her sorcery (1)

5 Glauce is killed by the magic robe presented to her by Medea (5)

6 Jason puts the dragon to sleep, takes possession of the Golden Fleece and departs with Medea (3)

FURNITURE

7 Pair of giltwood tables with marble tops and griffin supports by Tatham, Bailey & Sanders, 1814. Made for Carlton House.

8 Pair of giltwood tables with marble tops and sphinx supports, mid-18th century and later.

9 Two large circular tables by Morel & Seddon, with inlaid amboyna tops and winged-lion supports, c.1828.

10 Chinoiserie gilt-bronze clock and matching thermometer with painted bronze figures of a peacock and a Chinese man and woman. Supplied by Vulliamy for Brighton Pavilion, 1830.

11 Three massive English gilt-bronze and cut-glass chandeliers, c.1830.

12 Pieces from two suites of upholstered giltwood seat furniture (some with gilt-metal enrichments) by Morel & Seddon, 1828, covered with late 18th-century Beauvais tapestry. The set was extended for King George V and Queen Mary in the 1920s.

13 Aubusson flat-woven floral carpet with the cypher of King George V.

14 Two pairs of late 18th-century Chinese dark-blue porcelain vases, mounted as candelabra; the gilt-bronze chinoiserie mounts by the Vulliamys, 1819. From Brighton Pavilion.

15 Pair of Chinese blue porcelain candelabra with 18th-century French gilt-bronze mounts.

16 Pair of 18th-century Sèvres porcelain candelabra with gilt-bronze mounts.

17 Garnitures of late 18th-century French marble vases with gilt-bronze mounts.

SCULPTURE

18 Massive Russian urn veneered with malachite, presented to Queen Victoria by Tsar Nicholas I in 1839.

19 Bronze group of Louis XV supported on a shield, by Jean-Baptiste Lemoyne, 1776.

20 Bronze bust of the Prince de Condé, after Jérôme Derbais, early 18th century. Brought with no. 21 from Carlton House in 1828.

21 Bronze bust of Marshal Turenne after Jérôme Derbais, early 18th century.

22 Bronze bust of Cardinal Richelieu attributed to Jean Varin, 17th century.

23 Bronze bust of Charles I after Hubert Le Sueur, 18th century.

24 Bronze group of *The Abduction of Persephone by Pluto*, French, 18th century.

25 Bronze group of *Hercules, Antaeus and Gaea*, French, 18th century.

26 Bronze group of *Pluto and Persephone* after Girardon, French, 18th century.

27 Pair of bronze vases in the form of grotesque figures, French, 18th century.

Gobelins tapestry (detail): *Jason pledges his faith to Medea.*

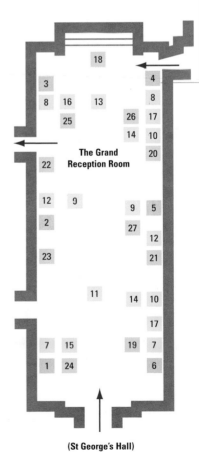

THE GARTER THRONE ROOM

THE GARTER THRONE ROOM WAS CREATED by Wyatville out of the first two of Charles II's state rooms, the King's Presence Chamber and the King's Privy or Audience Chamber; the shallow arch in front of the throne marks the line of the old wall between the two rooms. Wyatville removed Verrio's rich painted ceilings, which were deemed in bad condition, and replaced them with moulded plaster ceilings of his own design, ingeniously making use of the insignia and collar of the Order of the Garter, as he had already done elsewhere. Grinling Gibbons' seventeenth-century carved cornice survives or was copied, as does the wainscot of the dado, but the principal oak wall panels (together with the gilt wall lights and chandeliers) were inserted by Queen Mary in the early twentieth century to replace blue damask panels. The fine wood carvings are all reused from elsewhere; examples are the festoons over the fireplace surrounding a state portrait of The Queen and the delicate panels, incorporating the Garter Star, over the doors flanking the throne. The carved and gilt throne canopy was made originally for George III's Audience Chamber at Windsor. It is in this room that The Queen invests new Knights and Ladies of the Garter with the insignia of the Order, before their installation in St George's Chapel on Garter Day.

Louis Haghe, *Queen Victoria investing Louis-Philippe with the Garter, 11 October 1844*

PICTURES

1 Gainsborough Dupont, *George III*, 1795

2 Studio of Sir Thomas Lawrence, *George IV*, c.1818

3 Sir Martin Archer Shee, *William IV*, 1833

4 Sir James Gunn, *Queen Elizabeth II*, 1954–6

5 Franz Xaver Winterhalter, *Prince Albert*, 1843

6 Franz Xaver Winterhalter, *Queen Victoria*, 1843

7 Studio of Sir Godfrey Kneller, *George I*, c.1715

8 Sir Godfrey Kneller, *George II*, 1716

FURNITURE

9 Giltwood armchairs in the Gothic style designed by James Wyatt and made by John Russell and Charles Elliott, 1807.

10 Three giltwood pier tables, early 19th century.

11 Giltwood stools, late 18th century.

12 Giltwood throne canopy, late 18th century, with 19th-century velvet hangings.

13 Giltwood throne chair, made by White, Allom & Co. for the Coronation of Queen Elizabeth II, 1953.

14 Three giltwood chandeliers, copied from an 18th-century original at Hampton Court, 20th century.

PORCELAIN

15 Pair of Chinese powder-blue porcelain vases with French gilt-bronze mounts, mid-18th century. Purchased by Queen Mary in 1920.

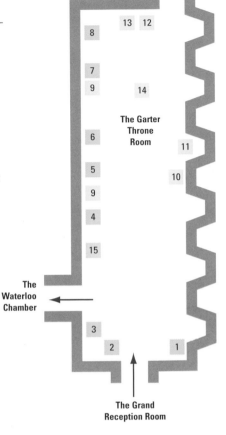

THE WATERLOO CHAMBER

ROOM PLAN ➤

THIS ROOM, DOMINATED BY THE PORTRAIT of the 1st Duke of Wellington, was conceived by George IV to commemorate the defeat of Napoleon at Waterloo in 1815. He commissioned portraits from Sir Thomas Lawrence of the Allied monarchs, statesmen and commanders who had contributed to the victory. Lawrence travelled round Europe to create this bravura series of more than twenty portraits.

It was part of Sir Charles Long's brief for the reconstruction of the castle that a setting be created for Lawrence's portraits, and for an annual banquet held on the anniversary of Waterloo on 18 June. Wyatville chose the larger of Edward III's inner courtyards – Horn Court – and roofed it over with an ingenious timber ceiling containing a raking clerestory that is reminiscent of ship's carpentry.

The panelling round the lower part of the room incorporates seventeenth-century wood carvings by Grinling Gibbons and his workshop which were salvaged from Charles II's demolished chapel. These include the palm fronds over the large doors at either end. The 'Elizabethan' fretted plaster decoration on the upper walls and the unusual glass chandeliers, by Osler, were added by Queen Victoria.

The room is used for the annual luncheon for the Knights of the Garter in June, when the table – decorated with silver-gilt, flowers, and porcelain from one of the historic services in the Royal Collection – is set for fifty to sixty guests. The room is also used for concerts and balls.

ABOVE: The cast of 'Old Mother Red Riding Boots' in the Waterloo Chamber, Windsor Castle, Christmas 1944. The Queen, when Princess Elizabeth, and Princess Margaret stand in the centre of the second row on the stage.

LEFT: The Waterloo Chamber prepared for a Garter Day lunch.

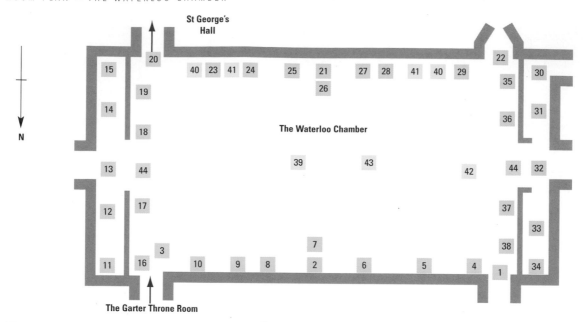

PICTURES

North Wall, Upper Row

1 Sir Thomas Lawrence, *Louis-Antoine, Duke of Angoulême,* 1825

2 William Corden, *Frederick William, Duke of Brunswick,* 1848

3 Sir Thomas Lawrence, *Prince Leopold of Saxe-Coburg, later King of the Belgians,* 1821

North Wall, Lower Row

4 Sir Thomas Lawrence, *Adolphus, Duke of Cambridge,* 1818

5 Sir Thomas Lawrence, *Robert Banks Jenkinson, 2nd Earl of Liverpool,* c.1820

6 Sir David Wilkie, *William IV,* 1832

7 Sir Thomas Lawrence, *George III,* c.1820

8 Studio of Sir Thomas Lawrence, *George IV,* c.1820

9 Sir Thomas Lawrence, *Robert Stewart, Viscount Castlereagh,* c.1817

10 Sir Thomas Lawrence, *Frederick, Duke of York,* 1816

East Wall, Upper Row

11 Robert McInnes, *General Sir James Kempt,* 1836

12 Sir Thomas Lawrence, *Matvei Ivanovitch, Count Platov,* 1814

13 Sir Thomas Lawrence, *Arthur Wellesley, 1st Duke of Wellington,* 1814–15

14 Sir Thomas Lawrence, *Field Marshal Gebhardt von Blücher,* 1814

15 James Lonsdale, *Sir William Congreve,* c.1805–10

East Wall, Lower Row

16 Sir Thomas Lawrence, *Charles William, Baron von Humboldt,* 1828

17 After Sir Thomas Lawrence, *George Canning,* c.1830

18 Sir Thomas Lawrence, *Henry, 3rd Earl Bathurst,* c.1820

19 Sir Thomas Lawrence, *Ernest Frederick, Count Münster,* 1820

South Wall, Upper Row

20 Sir Martin Archer Shee, *Henry Paget, 2nd Earl of Uxbridge and 1st Marquess of Anglesey,* 1836

21 Sir Thomas Lawrence, *Alexander Ivanovitch, Prince Chernichev,* 1818

22 Nicaise de Keyser, *William II, King of the Netherlands, when Prince of Orange,* 1846

South Wall, Lower Row

23 Sir Thomas Lawrence, *Ercole, Cardinal Consalvi,* 1819

24 Sir Thomas Lawrence, *Charles Augustus, Prince Hardenberg,* 1818

25 Sir Thomas Lawrence, *The Emperor Alexander I of Russia,* 1814–18

26 Sir Thomas Lawrence, *The Emperor Francis I of Austria,* 1818–19

27 Sir Thomas Lawrence, *Frederick William III of Prussia,* 1814–18

28 Sir Thomas Lawrence, *Charles Robert, Count Nesselrode,* 1818

29 Sir Thomas Lawrence, *Pope Pius VII,* 1819

West Wall, Upper Row

30 Henry William Pickersgill, *General Viscount Hill,* c.1830

31 Sir Thomas Lawrence, *Charles X of France,* 1825

32 Sir Thomas Lawrence, *Charles Philip, Prince Schwarzenberg,* 1819

33 Sir Thomas Lawrence, *Charles, Archduke of Austria,* 1819

34 Sir Martin Archer Shee, *Sir Thomas Picton,* 1836

West Wall, Lower Row

35 Sir Thomas Lawrence, *John, Count Capo D'Istria,* 1818–19

36 Sir Thomas Lawrence, *Clemens Lothar Wenzel, Prince Metternich,* 1819

37 Sir Thomas Lawrence, *Armand Emmanuel, Duke of Richelieu,* 1818

38 Sir Thomas Lawrence, *General Theodore Petrovitch Uvarov,* 1818

FURNITURE

39 Mahogany extending dining table by Thomas Dowbiggin, 1846.

40 Giltwood sofas in the Gothic style designed by James Wyatt and made by John Russell and Charles Elliot, 1807.

41 Two giltwood side tables with marble tops, 18th and 19th centuries.

42 Indian (Agra) carpet, presented to Queen Victoria in 1894.

43 Set of six French gilt-bronze tripod tazzas, early 19th century.

SCULPTURE

44 Limewood panels and drops, some by Grinling Gibbons and workshop.

THE QUADRANGLE

THE QUADRANGLE, WHICH CAN BE SEEN on leaving the state apartments, has provided the setting for many colourful ceremonies. When a foreign head of state pays a state visit he or she takes the salute here at a mounted rank past by the King's Troop, Royal Horse Artillery, followed by the Sovereign's Escort of the Household Cavalry and a march past of the Guard of Honour. When The Queen is in official residence the Changing of the Guard also takes place in the Quadrangle. By tradition, the Guard is frequently formed from a battalion of one of the Household regiments. Diagonally opposite is the Sovereign's Entrance, which gives access to the private royal apartments on the south and east sides. All along the south and east sides is the Grand Corridor, added by Wyatville for George IV, to improve communications between the different parts of the castle.

The bronze equestrian statue of Charles II was cast in 1679 by Josiah Ibach. It surveys the Quadrangle from the foot of the motte. Wyatville's granite plinth incorporates a small fountain and carved marble panels by Grinling Gibbons.

A rank past and march past for a state visit in the Quadrangle of Windsor Castle.

ST GEORGE'S CHAPEL

ST GEORGE'S CHAPEL LIES ON THE NORTH SIDE of the Lower Ward. Building work began under Edward IV in 1475 and the Quire, or choir, was completed by 1484, although with a wooden roof – very different from the magnificent fan vaulting seen by visitors today. This was added in the time of Henry VII, when the nave was also finished. The chapel was finally completed under Henry VIII in 1528, with the magnificent fan vault over the crossing.

Aside from its importance as the spiritual home of the Order of the Garter and the site of a number of royal tombs and memorials, the chapel ranks as one of the finest examples of the Perpendicular Gothic style of architecture in the country. This style was the final flowering of Gothic architecture in England, and is characterised by large windows, tall, slender pillars and an overall impression of soaring grace and elegance. Visitors to the chapel should take time to enjoy the sense of light and peace created by its architecture.

Features of note in the nave include the West Window, said to be the third largest in England. It is 11 metres (36 feet) high, and incorporates stained glass from the beginning of the 16th century. The nave also contains four chantry chapels. Chantry chapels were founded to employ priests to pray for the souls of their founders and their families. Royal tombs in the nave include that of King George V and Queen Mary, and the monument to Princess Charlotte, only child of George IV,

Stall plates of Knights of the Garter behind their seats in the Quire of St George's Chapel.

who died in childbirth in 1817 at the age of twenty-one. Her stillborn son is seen in the arms of the angel on the left.

Just past the northern entrance to the Quire is the King George VI Memorial Chapel, where King George VI, Queen Elizabeth The Queen Mother and Princess Margaret are interred. This chapel is not open to the public, but may be viewed from the north Quire aisle. Further royal tombs and memorials seen from the Quire include those of Edward IV, Henry VI, and of King Edward VII and Queen Alexandra. The vault of Henry VIII and Charles I is in the centre of the Quire.

Visitors can also see some remarkable examples of medieval wood- and ironwork. The west door of the original chapel (now the Albert Memorial Chapel), dating back to 1240, is preserved in the Ambulatory. The name of the maker, Gilbertus, is seen three times on its iron scrollwork. The seats in the 15th-century Quire stalls tip up to reveal carved misericords. The magnificent Sovereign's Stall was built in the late eighteenth century. It is used by The Queen when she attends the chapel.

OPPOSITE: St George's Chapel. Looking up the nave toward the Quire.

BELOW: The fan-vaulted ceiling of the Quire, with the banners of the Knights of the Order of the Garter.

A separate guidebook for St George's Chapel is also available.

The magnificent vaulted ceiling of the Albert Memorial Chapel.

As in Samuel Pepys' day (see page 41), the banners of the Knights of the Garter hang over their stalls in the Quire. There have been over 900 Knights, and among the exceptional features of St George's Chapel are the 670 decorated metal stall plates of past Knights of the Garter, which are fastened to the backs of the Quire stalls. The earliest, of c.1390, belonged to Lord Basset, and shows his cut-out crest of a black boar. A more recent addition is the stall plate of Sir Winston Churchill.

Some of the treasures of the chapel can also be seen as one leaves the Quire. These include Edward III's 2-metre- (6 foot) long sword, which is probably the weapon he wielded in battle, together with a likeness of the King, painted in 1615. Close by is an unusual wooden font dating from the 1600s. These are all in the south or 'Pilgrimage' aisle of the chapel, where visitors can still see a pilgrims' alms box, made c.1480 by John Tresilian to encourage pilgrims to the chapel to leave donations. As well as the tomb of Henry VI, who was noted for his piety, pilgrims also came to see the Schorne Chantry and the Cross Gneth. The Schorne Chantry was named in honour of John Schorne, a Buckinghamshire priest who died in 1314, and who had a reputation as a great healer of the sick. His body was brought to the chapel in 1481 and a shrine was built above it, but later replaced by the present tomb of the 1st Earl of Lincoln. The Cross Gneth boss, on the ceiling of the east end of the aisle, commemorates an elaborate reliquary presented to St George's by Edward III and said to have held a piece of the True Cross. The actual Cross Gneth may have stood in one of two niches near the boss, but was probably destroyed during the Reformation.

It is also usually possible for visitors to enter the Horseshoe Cloister, built around the west end of the chapel, and see where The Queen and the Knights of the Garter enter and leave St George's Chapel on Garter Day.

THE ALBERT MEMORIAL CHAPEL

THE RICHLY DECORATED INTERIOR of this fifteenth-century chapel, originally built as Henry III's chapel of 1240, was created by George Gilbert Scott for Queen Victoria to commemorate her husband Prince Albert, who died at Windsor in 1861. Although it is not open to the public it is possible for visitors to look inside and see the vaulted ceiling, with a gold mosaic by Antonio Salviati, and the inlaid marble panels by Henri de Triqueti around the lower walls which depict scenes from the Bible. The marble effigy of Prince Albert himself is also by Triqueti.

The Chapel is now dominated by Alfred Gilbert's masterpiece, the tomb of the Duke of Clarence and Avondale, the elder son of King Edward VII, who died in 1892.